EY LIBRARY

D0494343

Risk, social policy and welfare

Keighley College Library

T 5 0 7 3 7

Introducing Social Policy

Series Editor: David Gladstone

Risk, social policy and welfare

HAZEL KEMSHALL

Open University Press
Buckingham · Philadelphia

Open University Press
Celtic Court
22 Ballmoor
Buckingham
MK18 1XW

email: enquiries@openup.co.uk
world wide web: www.openup.co.uk

and
325 Chestnut Street
Philadelphia, PA 19106, USA

KEIGHLEY COLLEGE
LIBRARY
50737
-3 DEC 2004

First Published 2002

Copyright © Hazel Kemshall, 2002

All rights reserved. Except for the quotation of short passages for the
purpose of criticism and review, no part of this publication may be
reproduced, stored in a retrieval system, or transmitted, in any form
or by any means, electronic, mechanical, photocopying, recording or
otherwise, without the prior written permission of the publisher or a
licence from the Copyright Licensing Agency Limited. Details of such
licences (for reprographic reproduction) may be obtained from the
Copyright Licensing Agency Ltd of 90 Tottenham Court Road,
London W1P 0LP.

A catalogue record of this book is available from the British Library

ISBN 0 335 20409 0 (pb) 0 335 20410 4 (hb)

Library of Congress Cataloging-in-Publication Data
Kemshall, Hazel, 1958–
    Risk, social policy and welfare/Hazel Kemshall.
        p.   cm. – (Introducing social policy)
    Includes bibliographical references and index.
    ISBN 0-335-20410-4 – ISBN 0-335-20409-0 (pbk.)
    1. Great Britain–Social policy–1979– 2. Public welfare–Great Britain.
  3. Risk–Great Britain. I. Title. II. Series.

HN385.5 K45 2001
361.6′1′0941–dc21   2001021660

Typeset by Type Study, Scarborough
Printed in Great Britain by St Edmundsbury Press,
Bury St Edmunds, Suffolk

Contents

Series editor's foreword

Welcome to the third volume in the Introducing Social Policy series. The series itself is designed to provide a range of well informed texts on a wide variety of topics that fall within the ambit of social policy studies.

Although primarily designed with undergraduate social policy students in mind, it is hoped that the series – and individual titles within it – will have a wider appeal to students in other social science disciplines and to those engaged on professional and post-qualifying courses in health care and social welfare.

The aim throughout the planning of the series has been to produce a series of texts that both reflect and contribute to contemporary thinking and scholarship, and which present their discussion in a readable and easily accessible format.

In recent years, risk has become a central feature of analysis across a wide range of social science disciplines. The significance of Hazel Kemshall's present study lies in the relationship she identifies between risk and the reconfiguration of welfare. Drawing on much of the current theoretical literature, her opening chapter provides a well structured introduction to the risk society and an overview of its implications for social policy. Her specific argument is that risk is replacing need as the central principle of social policy formation and welfare delivery. She illustrates this contention in a succession of chapters relating to a variety of welfare sectors: health, child protection and the care of older people, and mental health provision, where she contrasts 'the exposure of a majority of mental health users to risk through social isolation, invisibility and neglect' with 'the intense regulation and surveillance of a high-risk minority deemed to pose a significant threat to public safety'.

Throughout the book she engages with current policy debates, especially those of positive welfare and the Third Way associated especially with

Anthony Giddens. But she also provides a cogent and critical discussion of much contemporary social policy legislation and the changing world of professional practice, in which risk management procedures now occupy a more established place in the new management of welfare.

In discussing risk, Hazel Kemshall provides a stimulating introduction to issues of theory, policy and practice and a lively and well informed discussion of its implication for the future of social policy and responsible citizenship. It is a book for anyone concerned with current directions in social policy and for the future shape of Britain's welfare arrangements.

David Gladstone, University of Bristol

Acknowledgements

Many friends and colleagues have supported me through the 'years of risk'. The instances of personal kindness and encouragement are too many to mention but my gratitude is heartfelt none the less.

Particular thanks go to Chris Neville for friendship and interest, Gill Mackenzie and Jacki Pritchard for professional advice and mentoring, my colleagues at DeMontfort University, and Paul Holt, Research Fellow. Thanks also go to David Gladstone, series editor, for his patience and advice, particularly in the early stages of writing this book. My initial project on risk was sponsored by the Economic and Social Research Council's 'Risk and Human Behaviour' programme grant number L211252018, 1994–7.

Introduction: risk, responsibility and social policy

Risk is 'big business' (Adams 1995) and it is certainly a risky business. Daily we are confronted with exhortations to take more care to avoid risks, and we are also held increasingly accountable for the risks we take. Our era is dominated by a peculiarly defensive attitude to risk, what Frank Furedi (1997) has labelled a 'culture of safety' in which risks are almost always framed by the precautionary principle of 'better safe than sorry'. This peculiarity of risk is exacerbated by increased personal responsibility for risk: risks are a matter of choice, governed by human agency, and not mere matters of accident or fate. All risks can be avoided: the prudent person should both risk assess and choose wisely. A key feature of risk in the 'risk society' is the meshing of risk, responsibility and prudent choice.

This book explores the interrelationship between risk and responsibility in contemporary social policy, and in particular the role of risk and responsibility in the construction and delivery of welfare provision. By drawing on key exemplars of provision in health, the personal social services and mental health, the book explores the growing relevance of risk and responsibility to the organization and delivery of welfare provision. The key contention is that risk, particularly an individualized and responsibilized risk, is replacing need as the core principle of social policy formation and welfare delivery. This is largely epitomized by 'Third Way' social policy responses to the 'risk society', but in the UK, for example, the key features of this trend are seen as predating the Blairite orthodoxy and to have implications beyond New Labour, currently in government.

The book is divided into six chapters. Chapter 1 introduces the contentious concepts of risk and social policy and endeavours to provide a working definition of each for the purposes of this volume. Risk is placed within a historical as well as contemporary context, and differing theoretical approaches to risk are explored. The rise of the risk society is outlined and implications for social policy are drawn. Chapter 2 examines broad social policy trends since the late 1970s to map the move from need to risk as a key organizing principle of welfare provision. Links between risk and individual responsibility are drawn, and the role of risk and prudentialism as key mechanisms of social regulation and governance in advanced liberal societies is explored.

Chapter 3 represents the first of the key exemplars and examines the role of risk and responsibilization in changing patterns of health care and health policy. Two key health policy themes – rationing and prevention – are explored. Chapter 4 examines the increasingly selective and residual provision of the personal social services with reference to child protection and care of the elderly. The reconstitution of need as risk and vulnerability in these two areas of social care provision is examined. Chapter 5 continues the theme of risk and residualism in community care provision through an examination of mental health policy and provision following deinstitutionalization of the asylums. The exposure of a majority of mental health users to risk through social isolation, invisibility and neglect is contrasted to the intense regulation and surveillance of a high-risk minority deemed to pose a significant risk to public safety. In this context, risk is used not only to classify users for a service, but also to introduce compulsory treatment and regulation for those constituted as a threat and also as unable to self-manage.

The final chapter concludes by returning to the broader conceptual context of the role of risk in social policy and welfare provision. The chapter considers whether a welfare consensus for the twenty-first century based on a risk-led 'positive welfare' (Giddens 1998a, b) can be discerned, and alternatives to Giddens's 'Third Way' are explored. Finally, the evidence for a transition from need to risk is considered.

Risk in contemporary society

Understanding risk: common usage and definitions

The word 'risk' is pervasive in contemporary life and has come to encompass a wide range of future events and behaviours that are often complex and far from uniform. In our personal lives we may ponder the risks of unemployment, health risks and crime, and the environmental risks of pollution. Despite the current odds of 14 million to one we may regularly risk the purchase of a lottery ticket and consider this a reasonable investment. On the other hand, we may over-estimate the odds of contracting bovine spongiform encephalopathy (BSE) and avoid the minimal risks of eating beef (*Daily Telegraph* 1997). In the former case we are prepared to be risk-takers despite the odds, and in the latter risk-avoiders in the face of low probability (Kemshall 1998). This example illustrates that risk decisions are about far more than simply 'calculating the odds'. The consequences of risks, and the acceptability or otherwise of the attendant impacts, are crucial in decisions about risk. As Lupton (1999: 59) expresses it, 'Debates and conflicts over risks have begun to dominate public, political and private arenas.'

Historical and contemporary use of risk

The word 'risk' is in common usage, but is difficult to define with precision (Adams 1995). In its early usage risk was value-neutral, concerned with the possibility of gain as well as loss, in, for example, gambling (Douglas 1992). In the eighteenth century risk became associated with marine insurance, the calculation of the chances of a ship returning safely to port or not and the notion of insuring against such loss (for example, with Lloyds of London); and later with the insurance of soldiers in the Napoleonic Wars (for example, with Scottish Widows). Personal knowledge and market forces rather than statistical calculations initially underpinned such insurance-based calculations of risk (Daston 1987). However, 'prudential insurance', as distinct from gambling, led to the development of a probability approach to risk (Green 1997: 147) and formal mathematical models of risk assessment came into use (Hacking 1987; Douglas 1992). This was supported by an expansion in numerical information and the mathematical identification of frequencies and averages within the population (Hacking 1987, 1990): in effect, the birth of statistics, essential for the risk calculations used by today's insurance actuaries.

Changes in the meaning and usage of the word risk can be traced to specific historical periods. Green (1997: 144) has outlined three main discourses in European thought: 'fate', 'determinism' and 'risk'. Pre-Renaissance thought was characterized by *fate*; that is, an explanatory system of personal misfortune and disaster based upon notions of chance and personal destiny. Risks were seen as the product of fate, destiny and the will of the Gods. Post-Renaissance thought was characterized by *determinism*; that is, explanatory systems based upon universal laws and causality. Risks were seen as the products of such determinism and the vagaries of nature. The era of *actuarial* or *insurance* risk is rooted in probability thinking and the rise of science and mathematics. The language of probability has contributed much to the field of risk (Bernstein 1996), facilitating the twentieth-century framing of risk within engineering and scientific discourse as a statistically calculable hazard. This approach was given added impetus by twentieth-century concerns with the high-consequence risks associated with the nuclear industry and the desire to prevent hazardous accidents (Douglas 1986). The 'vagaries of nature' were recast as statistical probability. This is the era labelled by Hacking (1987: 54) as the 'taming of chance'.

This actuarial, technically based understanding of risk has its roots within 'modernity', defined by Giddens (1991: 14–15) as the process and institutions of industrialization. Rationality and objective, scientific knowledge are endemic to modern thinking (Douglas 1992). Within this framing of risk the social as well as the natural world 'may be measured, calculated and therefore predicted' (Lupton 1999: 6). In addition, fate is replaced by human agency. The actions and activities of humans give rise to risks rather than the will of the Gods (Giddens 1990); for example, the risks of unemployment resulting from economic change, or the risks to health from industrial waste. During the nineteenth and twentieth centuries the probability and statistical calculations of actuarial risk were applied to many aspects of social life and public policy. The extension of commercial insurance to almost every aspect of social life is one example (Rowe 1977), and in social policy the application of a publicly funded insurance system for health and unemployment is another (the Health Service and National Insurance, respectively). Both these latter examples are responses to external risks, risk from the 'outside', which 'happen regularly enough and often enough in a whole population of people to be broadly predictable, and so insurable' (Giddens 1998a: 27). For Giddens collective insurance against external risks is a key feature of the welfare state in post-1945 Britain (Giddens 1998b).

Late modernity, or postmodernity as it is sometimes called (Giddens 1991; Smart 1993), has challenged this 'myth of calculability' (Reddy 1996: 237). Recent commentators such as Beck and Giddens have argued that post-modernity can be characterized by global risks, indeterminate and contingent knowledge about the probability of such risks, and uncertainty over future outcomes and impacts (Giddens 1991, 1994, 1998a, b; Beck 1992a, b, 1996, 1998). This is what Giddens in his 1999 Reith lectures labelled the 'runaway world' (Giddens 1999). This world is characterized by internally produced or manufactured risks, in contrast to the external risks of the natural world. These risks are seen as the very products of science and tech-nology, with the attendant 'advances' producing as many uncertainties and risks as they are intended to resolve (Giddens 1998a: 28). There are always unintended side effects and consequences; hence public disquiet over gene-tically modified foods. As Giddens expresses it: 'We just cannot know beforehand when we are actually "scaremongering" and when we are not' (Giddens 1998a: 30). The expansion of choice and the dissolution of tradi-tional norms and social bonds exacerbate this situation (Beck 1992a, b; Giddens 1998a, b). Technology itself expands the range of individual choice, through, for example, the development of Internet information and 'e-commerce'. Customary patterns of responding to the world are subse-quently challenged: 'As customary ways of doing things become problematic, people must choose in many areas which used to be governed by taken-for-granted norms' (Giddens 1998a: 30).

However, postmodernity 'offers little help as to which options should be selected' (Giddens 1991: 80). This can raise the personal anxiety stakes con-siderably. As the traditional bonds of social class and family are superseded by the 'new dependencies' of 'fashions, social policy, economic cycles and markets' the individual is increasingly exposed to risk (Beck 1992a: 131). Getting risk right is down to individual calculation and the types of choices which are made. This can be highly anxiety provoking and requires a high degree of self-monitoring or *reflexivity* to manage successfully. As Giddens expresses it, 'People have to take a more active and risk-infused orientation to their relationships and involvements' (Giddens 1998a: 28).

Is there a 'risk society'?

The transformation of modernity into 'late' or 'post' modernity has led commentators such as Beck to argue that we are living in a 'risk society' (Beck 1992a, 1996, 1998). In brief, Beck argues that the conditions of late modernity itself are now producing risks as well as benefits, 'the hazards and insecurities induced and introduced by modernisation itself' (Beck 1992a: 21). For Beck, risk society begins where nature and tradition end. Concern has shifted from naturally occurring and imposed external risks, to those risks generated by the very processes of industrialization and modernization. Traditional securities are superseded by risk choices and the individual's life course is characterized by uncertainty. Thus, individuals' life experience is characterized by their exposure to and successful navigation of risk. The central preoccupation of risk society is no longer with the distribution of wealth, but with the distribution of risks, who manufactures them and upon whom they fall. While Beck argues that disadvantaged groups are likely to experience the highest degrees of risk and have the least resources to manage them successfully, in risk society we are all exposed to some degree.

However, other commentators have argued that Beck's (1998: 12) 'manufactured uncertainty' is over-stated (Steuer 1998). These critiques tend to focus on three points from Beck's thesis:

- risks are under-regulated, and the social control previously imposed upon technology is now absent;
- the end of traditional bonds exacerbates risk;
- risks have increased.

Is risk under-regulated?

Risk assessment and risk management have gained an increased significance in many spheres, including social care and social policy. Risk failures attract attention, and in the case of major risk failures such as the Challenger shuttle disaster, the Brent Spar debate, the failure of Barings Bank, the death in care of children, and food risk scandals, attention shifts to blame, accountability and systems of regulation. Failures quickly focus attention on the very systems designed to regulate risk and deliver risk control; further failures must be prevented. Nuclear power is of course a key example. However, as both Giddens (1990, 1991) and Beck (1992a, b) argue, it is not merely a case that new or increased risks require further systems of regulation, or that technology is necessarily out of control. The key issue is that systems of regulation can themselves inadvertently produce the very risks they are required to control and minimize. A recent example is the fail-safe procedures at the Chernobyl nuclear power plant that led to a nuclear discharge (Wildavsky 1988). Fail-safe procedures rarely are, and risk control systems can atrophy as vigilance falls, a position well illustrated by the Piper Alpha oil rig fire (Cullen 1990).

There is also growing recognition that social and economic changes themselves produce risks and that such risks can be transnational (e.g. environmental risks like acid rain), and they therefore require diverse systems of regulation in addition to the traditional regulation of state government.

These diverse systems can include corporate regulation, self-regulation and regulation by non-government organizations, in addition to the regulation of supra-national bodies such as the European Union. Other commentators such as Hood (1996) have argued that the issue is not necessarily one of more regulation but, instead, of the types of regulation and risk management systems that should be used. Central to this issue is the question of compliance and the implementation of risk management systems in arenas where risks may be contested and differently understood. The disposal of the Brent Spar oil rig by Shell in 1995 is a key example. In this case the risk of environmental contamination was differently defined and estimated by Greenpeace and Shell, a difference which Wilkinson (1997), analysing the situation for Shell, attributed to the difference in the value frames of Greenpeace and Shell. While the disposal plan had expert and government endorsement, it was strongly resisted by Greenpeace and public outrage soon followed. Shell had significantly underestimated the value-laden nature of risk judgements, and in particular the role of trust in accepting or resisting risk management systems and risk regulation:

> Trust is a critical factor in bridging the differences between our different 'world views' . . . A common starting point in our developing approach to wider engagement and communications has been to re-establish and continue to build trust-based relationships.
>
> (Wilkinson 1997: 940)

Trust and engagement have been recognized as key features of any risk regulation system if it is to work (Wynne 1992; Wilkinson 1997). This has resulted in more recent attention to regulatory systems which can resolve risk conflicts, promote trust and engagement, adapt to change and operate flexibly as risks change (Collingbridge 1992, 1996; Hood 1996).

The end of traditional bonds?

In their work *Young People and Social Change: Individualization and Risk in Late Modernity*, Furlong and Cartmel (1997) place Beck's (1998: 12) contention that 'risk begins where tradition ends' in context. While traditional bonds may be weakening, and other post-industrialization forces are coming into play, Beck (1992a: 35) has argued that risks are likely to be distributed within society along existing lines of inequality. The key difference for Beck (1992a: 131) is that class position can no longer be used to predict a person's life course as differing choices can be made about 'lifestyles, subcultures, social ties and identities'. From substantial research into the social conditions of young people, Furlong and Cartmel dispute this claim. For many, and especially for Furlong and Cartmel's young people, life chances remain severely restricted. The difference now is that risks are framed, experienced and negotiated individually, and consequently collective identities are weakened. 'Public issues' are literally transformed into 'private troubles' (Wright Mills 1970). Failure to negotiate a risk adequately is rewritten as an individual failure rather than understood as a result of social processes outside the individual's control. The danger of such individualization is that social inequalities remain hidden and collective responses are delegitimated.

Have risks increased?

Adams (1995: 179) argues that Beck's distinction between modern risk and traditional dangers is 'somewhat exaggerated'. While modern risks may be characterized by their global scale and invisibility, for Adams this does not necessarily make them new. He contends, for example, that the risk of deadly disease has always existed, the difference is science's ability to 'discover' such risks. Indeed, the invisible causes of risks led pre-Renaissance societies to frame such risks as matters of fate or acts of God, and the bubonic plague can be understood as an early example of a global risk spread by the expansion of shipping and trade.

So, as Beck puts it: 'Aren't all risks at least as old as industrial society, possibly even as old as the human race itself? Isn't all life subject to the risk of death? Aren't and weren't all societies in all epochs "risk societies"?' (Beck 1992b: 97). Is risk society a new phenomenon? Have risks increased and are there new risks? Certainly Beck argues for the multiplicity of risks:

> There occurs, so to speak, an over-production of risks, which sometimes relativize, sometimes supplement and sometimes outdo one another. One hazardous product might be defended by dramatizing the risks of the others (for example, the dramatization of climatic consequences 'minimizes' the risk of nuclear energy.
>
> (Beck 1992a: 31)

While it may be difficult to establish whether risks have increased, these risks do have new features. They are usually global in scale, and characterized by low probability but high consequence (for example, the risk of nuclear discharge). They are also indiscriminate in their impact: everyone is potentially 'at risk'. Perhaps more importantly, they also have their origins in the political and organizational processes of decision-making on risk, attributable to human agency rather than to fate (Beck 1992b: 98). These risks result from human decisions, not from acts of God. The location of risks in the social, economic and political processes of modernization increases the individual's exposure to risk. Is it any wonder, therefore, that we see risk everywhere? Such risks are also less forgivable than those imposed by fate. If caused by organizational failings and human agency, then surely they are predictable and preventable. As Green (1997) puts it: accidents happen, but risks are caused. Beck's risks are blameworthy. A key feature of risks in late modernity is liability and accountability. Someone must be to blame, someone must be held to account, someone must pay (Douglas 1992).

The precautionary principle and risk prevention

Risks have consequences for the future as well as for the present. The future impact of industrially produced risks is incalculable: we won't know the consequences until we get there and experience them. This results in a pre-occupation with the 'precautionary principle' (Tait and Levidow 1992) and a defensive concern to be 'safe rather than sorry'. This is often expressed in media and public concerns over risk; for example, BSE, *E. coli*, genetically modified foods and sexual abuse of children. Such concern can be 'at odds' with the statistical likelihood of their occurrence (Kemshall 1999). Uhlig, discussing the issue in the *Daily Telegraph*, noted that the risk of contracting variant Creutzfeld-Jakob disease (CJD) by eating beef on the bone is calculated as one in six million, in contrast to the likelihood of dying from smoking ten cigarettes a day (*Daily Telegraph* 1997). Similarly, children are more likely to be sexually abused or murdered by parents than by strangers, yet 'stranger-danger' has dominated both public reaction and public policy responses (Wyre 1997; Kitzinger 1999). The result is a society 'defensive' about risk, concerned with risk avoidance and the prevention of harms, even harms not yet known and incalculable without future knowledge (Beck 1992a). In such a climate risks tend to be framed negatively in terms of harms to be avoided.

Risk and blame

Negative risks and exposure to risks inevitably raise the spectre of blame, or what Mary Douglas (1992: 27) has called the 'forensic functions' of risk. She expresses the contemporary preoccupation with blame thus:

> the [system] we are in now is almost ready to treat every death as chargeable to someone's account, every accident as caused by someone's criminal negligence, every sickness a threatened prosecution. Whose fault? is the first question.
>
> (Douglas 1992: 15–16)

Attribution of blame and fault necessarily focuses attention on accountability for risk assessment and management. This results in the strange paradox that as risks become increasingly unknowable and incalculable, formalized systems for assessing and managing risks grow (Kemshall *et al.* 1997). Individuals and organizations charged with getting risk right are required to defend these decisions, often from litigation, and formalized assessment methods are used to replace the vagaries of professional judgement (Kemshall *et al.* 1997). This has been particularly acute in welfare, health, social care and criminal justice, as well as the more traditional risk arenas of science, engineering and new technologies. As Kemshall *et al.* (1997) express it, audit, formalized assessment and bureaucratic risk management systems have become a key response to the uncertainty of risk.

Summary

Common usage and definitions of risk have changed through the ages. This section has reviewed the historical journey of risk from the acceptance of fate to the contemporary understanding of risk as 'manufactured uncertainty'. At the beginning of the twenty-first century we are in a transition stage – not only from modernity to late or postmodernity, but also from the certain language of risk as probability to risk as uncertainty, from calculable external risks to incalculable internally generated risks. Key responses to this transition have paradoxically been a retreat into formalized, actuarially based risk systems, and a defensive attitude to risk which emphasizes caution, accountability and risk management.

Approaches to risk: theories and methods

Risk is big business, and the risk industry is growing. Indeed, Adams (1995: 31) has labelled it the 'world's largest industry'. Risks are no longer confined to natural hazards, or external sources of threat, but have their source in social change, economic forces, scientific development and technological change. They are even initiated by the very institutions and regulatory systems set up to manage risk (for example, regulatory systems for toxic or nuclear waste, and recent bureaucratic systems to identify and manage sex offenders). The range of risks confronting us is incredibly diverse. The contemporary challenge is how to understand and successfully to navigate such risks.

Approaches to risk

The Royal Society Study Group on risk took up this challenge in 1983 and subsequently in 1992. The latter report represented something of a watershed in approaches to risk. The 1983 report had framed risk in entirely objective terms, using the discourse of probability from science and engineering. By 1992 the Society felt the need to include two chapters from social scientists to address risk perception and the social context. The report epitomized the dawning recognition of the consequences of late modernity for understanding risk, particularly of the importance of risk perception, differing views of risk and risk as a future uncertainty. The report is, however, located within modern rather than late or postmodern thinking. While the report accepted the notion of subjective risks – that is differing perceptions of risks across individuals and groups – the Society's main concern remained the identification and regulation of objectively knowable and calculable risks. Along with studies of the 'risk society', this objective–subjective divide in understanding risk has preoccupied much of the subsequent research (Economic and Social Research Council 1993).

Theorizing risk: the two cultures

Traditionally risk research had been the preserve of engineers and natural scientists concerned with technological risks and natural hazards. Such research tended to adopt an 'artefact' approach to risk, framing risk as a static, objective reality amenable to measurement and probabilistic calculation (Horlick-Jones 1998). Within the social realm this approach has been represented by the psychometric tradition using the disciplines of cognitive psychology and decision theory to investigate individual risk decisions and choices. The paradigm has been concerned with the correction of poor risk choices – for example, drug taking, drink-driving, alcohol abuse – in an effort to inform individual risk decisions and to improve the efficacy of public risk campaigns. The paradigm poses the risk assessor as *Homo prudens*, epitomized by 'prudence, rationality and responsibility' (Adams 1995: 16), and the focus is upon why expert risk information is ignored or disregarded, resulting in 'irrational' decision-making.

Limitations to this approach have been increasingly recognized (Rayner 1992; Jasanoff 1993; Adams 1995). Adams has refuted *Homo prudens*, noting that risks can lead to rewards (hence some of us gamble), and that risky behaviours can be actively sought (for example, bungee jumping for the thrill). Despite Beck's risk society people are risk takers as well as avoiders. Risks can also change over time and across contexts. Risks that are acceptable today may not be tomorrow. Young risk-taking motorcycle drivers usually become old risk-avoiding car drivers (Bellaby 1990), and the risks we take in our private lives are not always the risks we take at work. Risk is not always a matter of individual choice: peer group pressure and social interaction have long been noted as key features of drug and alcohol use (Bloor 1995), and choice can be constrained by lack of power and opportunity (Kemshall 1998). These limitations have moved the focus of analysis away from the individual to the group and to society.

Social theories of risk

Social theories of risk emphasize the context within which decisions are made and locate individual risk decision-making within the social realm. Under the broad rubric of socially constituted views of risk, the paradigm actually has a number of differing constituents. In brief these are:

- Investigations of the subjective perception of risk, and why lay publics fail to act upon expert advice. Subjective processes are seen as important, but the objective reality of risk is taken as the norm. The aim of such research is essentially corrective (for example, Slovic 1992). In effect, much of this work belongs within the materialist, psychometric paradigm, and attention to the 'social' is merely in passing.
- Cultural theory, on the other hand, poses that 'Risk is always a social product (Thompson and Wildavsky 1982: 148). Cultural theory has been particularly important in investigating the relationship between values, beliefs and risk perception. Mary Douglas's work in particular has been influential in examining the connection between membership of a group and one's view of the world on the one hand, and perceptions of risk on the other (Douglas 1992). The other key theoretical contribution of cultural theory has been the examination of how risks are selected for concern and how these risks are legitimated for public attention. In essence, the argument is that risks are chosen for their usefulness to the social system, whether that be tribal taboos or the moral panics of the twentieth century (Douglas 1992). They contribute to social cohesion and distinctions between 'insiders' and 'outsiders'.
- Social constructivism has similar concerns to cultural theory and treats risk as a socially constructed phenomenon determined by social processes. This approach stresses the role of the social in the construction of risk meanings and their legitimacy, and emphasizes that a multiplicity of meanings and perception on risk can exist. Research focuses on the context of risk decisions, and the knowledge and social processes that contribute to the formulation of risk concerns and their perception. Disputes over risk levels or differences over the acceptability of risks (e.g. nuclear power or environmental risks) are understood as disputes of value and meaning. The Greenpeace dispute with Shell over the disposal of the Brent Spar (Wilkinson 1997) and/or clashes of view between sheep farmers and Ministry of Agriculture experts on the impact of radiation contamination post-Chernobyl are recent examples (Wynne 1996). In the latter case expert estimations of contamination were inaccurate, as ministry officials failed to take account of both local geographical factors and local farming practices, but it was the experts' view which counted and informed subsequent policy.

Conflicting discourses of risk

The varying social theories of risk have focused attention on the plurality of meaning often found in the use of the term 'risk', and upon conflicts of view about the nature and extent of risks. This is usually expressed in research terms as disputes or conflicts between differing *discourses* of risk. Lupton usefully defines discourse as 'a bounded body of knowledge and associated practices, a particular identifiable way of giving meaning to reality via words or imagery' (Lupton 1999: 15).

Discourse not only facilitates our understanding of the world, it also limits our perception and understanding of the phenomena around us, including social processes, social institutions and cultural forms. As Lupton (1999: 15) puts it, 'it may be said that there are a series of discourses on risk that serve to organize the ways in which we perceive and deal with risk'. The fatalistic approach to risk pre-Renaissance outlined by J. Green (1997) was one example of a risk discourse. Hacking's (1987, 1990) taming of chance and the discourse of risk as probability subsequently superseded this. In late modernity (or postmodernity) it is possible to identify the emergence of another risk discourse: risk as uncertainty. At the beginning of the twenty-first century it is possible to see both the discourse of probability and the discourse of uncertainty exemplified in responses to risk. The public debate over the introduction of genetically modified (GM) foods is a key example. In this case, both government and the company responsible for GM technology frame potential risk as a matter of clearly calculated probabilities, and on these grounds present the possible risk to the public as minimal. Potential risks to the environment are seen as risks which should be established through scientifically controlled trials in which appropriate data can inform risk calculations. Until the statement by the Prime Minister in which he argued for a degree of caution in the use of GM foods (*Independent on Sunday* 2000), government statements had tended to reinforce this scientific view.

On the other hand, media attention and public disquiet have tended to focus on the incalculable nature of such risks and the difficulty in calculating the full range of potential consequences until it is too late (*Horizon* 2000). Central to such disquiet is lack of trust in those experts calculating and managing such risks, in this case the company concerned. Views of risk and its subsequent calculation are seen as driven by vested interest and as therefore inherently untrustworthy (Freudenberg 1988, 1993). Experts no longer occupy the high ground, particularly as they often contradict each other, and expert views can be 'at odds' with the experiences of 'lay persons' (Wynne 1996). This was supported by Wilkinson's (1997) study of the Brent Spar disposal by Shell. These perceptions and questions of acceptability are not then merely a matter of 'calculating the odds'. If this were so, most of us would not purchase a lottery ticket as the current odds of winning are estimated at 14 million to one. Similarly, some of us will not eat beef for fear of BSE but continue to smoke 40 cigarettes a day. Whatever our risk choice, we are likely to justify it and to consider it as both rational and reasonable, and indeed we may feel threatened and disregarded when our view of risk is challenged. As Lupton puts it, to those expressing their view of risk, it has its 'own logic and rationale, and makes eminent sense . . . as part of their views on life' (Lupton 1999: 106).

Governments also make risk choices and display their risk discourse in the framing of public policy. In recent years this has been exemplified by government responses to a range of risks, most notably BSE, *E. coli*, GM foods and paedophile risks to children. With the exception of GM foods, government response has adopted the precautionary principle, with risk framed as both contingent and uncertain, in effect a late modern discourse of risk amplified by media attention and public concern. The BSE and *E. coli* outbreaks were characterized by high public anxiety, scepticism of expert opinion and diminished trust in risk management institutions (Miller and Reilly 1996). However, both responses were somewhat at odds with the known statistically calculated levels of risk (Miller and Reilly 1996; Eldridge *et al.* 1997). The increased regulation of paedophiles and sex offenders in the community is a further example. This has resulted in extensive legislation to control and regulate sex offenders in the community (Home Office 1997, 1998), although 'stranger-danger' is recognized as a statistically lower risk than familial sex abuse of children (Wyre 1997; Kitzinger 1999). In other areas of public policy a calculated and probabilistic discourse is more evident. This is particularly acute in those areas where resources are limited; for example, health, social care and criminal justice. Commentators have noted the rise of 'actuarial practices' in such areas (Simon 1987); that is, an increasingly insurance approach to risk in which risks are aggregated and statistically calculated, and individuals are represented as 'instances of a population' (p. 62). Individuals then gain access to services on the basis of their risk level, or risks are calculated in order to prevent them (for example, the prevention of health risks through public health campaigns). Simon traces this actuarial preoccupation through the development of accident insurance (for example, workers insuring against the calamity of disabling accidents), welfare state provision to cover the risks of the general population, the legal liability of companies for their products, health care and medical malpractice, to more recent developments in insurance for cars and credit cards, personal insurance and privately organized systems for guarding against crime risks.

The actuarial practices of probabilistic risk discourse are well embedded in societal responses to risk. However, these are increasingly challenged by a risk discourse of uncertainty as the potential future impact of some risks (particularly those arising from new technologies) remains incalculable. Probabilistic calculations of risks occurring and the cost–benefit assessments that usually accompany them are also open to dispute. Lack of trust in those making the calculations, disregard for expert opinion and conflicting knowledges and perceptions of risk undermine pure calculations of the odds. Late modernity can therefore be characterized by this conflict and transition in risk discourses (Giddens 1991, 1998a, b).

Summary

The probability discourse of risk was epitomized by science and engineering in the twentieth century. However, social theories of risk and the location of risk in the social realm have seriously challenged this 'artefact' view of risk. This new avenue of research has focused attention upon the diversity of risk perceptions and meanings current in social life. While probabilistic discourse is still prevalent in much government policy, public scepticism and diminished trust in risk policies and their risk regulation regimes is presenting severe challenges to the actuarial discourse of risk. Risk as calculable probabilities is being displaced by risk as future uncertainty.

Risk and social policy

Defining social policy is almost as problematic as defining risk. As Lavalette and Pratt (1997: 5) express it, 'social policy can be seen as an intensely political project and . . . an immensely important arena in which competing ideologies can clash'. Social policy is as prey to definitional dispute and value framing as risk, and as such is a contested area of study. Lavalette and Pratt suggest that one way out of this definitional mire is to consider social policy as concerned with the state organization of social provision, although this provision may differ in its nature and extent, and in the type of state organization that provides it. For them it is a given that most countries 'modify the operation of market forces in the allocation of health, housing, education, income maintenance and the personal social services' (p. 3). Social policy as a discipline can therefore be defined as the study of the organization and delivery of social provision in a range of forms. Social policy as a practice has long been associated with social democratic societies and a commitment to meet social need outside of market forces (Titmuss 1968, 1974), although this has recently been seen as a rather restricted view (Lavalette and Pratt 1997). Developments since the early 1980s have seen the rise of mixed economies of welfare and the increasing use of the market for social provision in social democratic societies (Mooney 1997). In addition, Lavalette and Pratt (1997: 5) remind us that social policy can also be central to policies of social control, at a benign level 'sentencing' people to welfare control and intrusion, and at its extreme used in Nazi Germany to eradicate whole populations. This use of social policy also suggests that it is part of a planned and intended strategy of wider public policy, the distinction between mere eclectic social programmes and a broader 'organizing totality' instrumentally used for political ends. This defines social policy as an intensely political as well as ideological enterprise.

The postmodern transformation of social policy and welfare provision

Leonard (1997: 1) has argued that the 'state's retreat' from welfare provision and the attendant changes in the pattern of social policy are now self-evident in Western societies. Numerous commentators have identified the 'Thatcher years' and the rise of the 'New Right' in the 1980s as central to this rolling back of the welfare state, and the strategic use of social policy in this era to achieve a reconstruction of welfare has been well documented (Deakin 1987; Clarke *et al.* 1994; Clarke and Newman 1997; Lavalette and Pratt 1997). Mooney (1997) for example, has noted the rise of the market and the mixed economy of welfare as a strategic tool in the reconfiguration of the health and personal social services. These developments have often been paralleled by increased attention to management objectives and style, epitomized by the new managerialism of 'key performance indicators' and the slogan 'the right to manage' (Clarke *et al.* 1994). Managerialism was promoted as a way to introduce sound business practices into the ailing and profligate bureaucracies of the welfare state, and was seen as an effective vehicle of organizational change.

Commentators identify three main strands in the New Right transformation of the welfare state:

- the growing and unsustainable economic costs of welfare provision and the restrictive impact this was seen as having upon private sector wealth creation;
- the political and ideological wish to reduce state intervention and individual dependency upon the 'nanny state';
- reduction in the power of the welfare state and the public sector, particularly as a site of opposition to government power (Clarke *et al.* 1994: 21–2; see also: Deakin 1987; Clarke and Newman 1997; Lavalette and Pratt 1997).

The new global economy has been posed as a particular consideration in the reconstruction of welfare (Jessop 1993, 1994, 2000), with the contention that the global market requires post-Fordist organizational forms in order to function efficiently. While Jessop acknowledges that there are real issues in applying both Fordism and post-Fordism to analyses of welfare and state reconstruction, his work does draw attention to significant transformations in the late modern capitalist state. For Jessop, Fordism can be understood as a particular form of labour organization dominated by mass production processes to serve mass consumption, supported by notions of collective bargaining and a Keynesian welfare state to regulate the needs of the workforce. For Jessop, Fordist states are characterized by social cohesion and a mode of social regulation that supports and legitimates capitalist production and consumption (Jessop 1993: 14–15).

Fordist states have been challenged by the 'rise of new technologies', 'growing internationalisation' and 'the regionalisation of global and national economies' (Jessop 1993: 25). Increasingly the global market supersedes the boundaries of the national market, and the traditional capitalist economies are challenged by the competitiveness of the newly industrialized countries. Constant innovation, technological development and flexibility of production and supply are central to maintaining a competitive edge. The post-Fordist state can be characterized by:

- flexibility of labour market and production;
- technological innovation;
- economic regulation based upon an enterprise culture and the reward of flexible technological skills rather than traditional collective bargaining;
- leaner organizational forms designed to deliver flexible supply systems (Jessop 1993: 19–20).

Jessop argues that this has resulted in 'a structural transformation and fundamental strategic reorientation of the capitalist state' (p. 24) from a 'Keynesian welfare state' to a 'Schumpeterian workfare state', with the latter geared to the facilitation of market innovation and flexibility in labour processes and supply. While useful for its attention to significant economic impacts upon the configuration of the state and welfare provision, Jessop's analysis is not without its critics. Clarke and Newman (1997) have argued that post-Fordist analysis does not necessarily transpose to the social policy arena. They argue that universal welfare provision cannot readily be equated with mass production, and that the professional discretion exercised by state welfare workers is more reminiscent of pre-Fordist craft production than the imposition of mass production techniques (Cochrane 1993). While they accept that there have been significant processes of restructuring 'between the state and the citizen; between the state and the economy; and between the state and institutional and organisational forms' (Clarke and Newman 1997: 24), this is not simply a matter of post-Fordist transformation and the impact of the global economy.

Leonard (1997: 1) also takes issue with the predominance of economic explanations for the 'retreat of the welfare state'. He locates changes within modes of welfare provision in broader 'discourses of welfare', in which social and cultural changes are seen as equally important to the processes of transformation as economic ones. He places what Jessop has termed the 'Keynesian welfare state' within the discourse of modernity, a discourse which emphasized: the 'Golden Age' of progress; reason and knowledge as the foundations of rational interventions for the individual and public good; and social reform through enlightened social policy and professional expertise. Leonard identifies the period from the Second World War to the mid-1970s as the major expression of this discourse in

Britain, allied to the dominance of a social democratic conception of the state. It was a period in which universal welfare was seen as ameliorating the worst excesses of capitalism, and ever-expanding social reform was viewed as the means of improving the life-chances of the whole population.

While Leonard does not underplay the impact of economic change, his analysis importantly links changes in social policy and welfare provision to the broader cultural and social changes embedded in the transition from modernity to postmodernity. His analysis can briefly be reviewed in terms of the following key themes:

- *The certainties of modernity's knowledge and truth claims are increasingly under challenge.* Within welfare provision, for example, the expertise of professionals is increasingly challenged by user groups, and the ethics and efficacy of interventions implemented on behalf of the public or individual good are questioned.
- *The social control function of welfare provision is both recognized and questioned.* Welfare as 'discipline' has received great attention since Foucault's ground breaking work (Foucault 1965, 1973), and sentencing to welfare dependency has been heavily critiqued (Murray 1990). The role of the state in monitoring and controlling populations to protect existing sites of power is now widely accepted (Foucault 1977). The welfare agenda under modernity is therefore characterized as a vehicle of oppression as well as a vehicle of progress.
- *The inclusive and life-enhancing project of modernity has not entirely fulfilled its early promise.* Certain groups, particularly women and ethnic minorities, remain marginalized, and welfare provision reinforces rather than removes their exclusion. As Leonard (1997: 25) expresses it, social inclusion is promoted at the expense of the excluded 'Other', the 'bad mothers', the 'work-shy' and the 'spongers'. The 'Oneness' of universal welfare provision is quick to collapse under the 'brute reality of economic recession' and the 'ever-deepening dichotomies of rich/poor, employed/unemployed, male/female, white/black'.
- *The certainty of modernity is itself challenged, resulting in a loss of faith in Reason, and public scepticism and doubt about existing social and political forms.* Traditional forms and the old universals cannot be taken for granted. As Leonard (1997: 22) puts it, we are living in 'New Times'.

Summary

The impact of structural, economic and social changes upon social welfare has been profound. The underpinning rationale of welfare provision as a major mechanism for the provision of progress and social improvement can no longer be taken for granted. Other forms and rationales can be countenanced, epitomized by a Labour Prime Minister (Blair 1997) asking the minister responsible for welfare provision to 'think the unthinkable'. Late modernity, or indeed postmodernity, is posing severe challenges to existing forms of social policy and welfare provision. Predominant among these challenges is the need to manage adequately the transition to a post-Fordist global economy, coupled with a growing disillusionment in the ability of traditional forms of welfare to promote the collective good. The 'Old Universals' no longer command uncritical confidence and respect. The key issue now is how social policy and welfare provision can and should respond to the risk society.

Social policy in the risk society

Giddens (1998b) has argued that the state's responsibility for risk management is more extensive than ever before. While the state was traditionally responsible for the effective management of economic risks through the collective provision of the welfare state and the efficient regulation of the market economy, its responsibility for risk now encompasses those risks arising from globalization, science and technology (Giddens 1998b: 76). Indeed, Giddens suggests that:

> In a society such as ours, oriented towards the future and saturated with information, the theme of risk unites many otherwise disparate areas of politics: welfare state reform, engagement with world financial markets, responses to technological change, ecological problems and geopolitical transformations.
>
> (Giddens 1998b: 64)

He urges us to be 'bold' in our responses to these new risk dilemmas in order to 'confront and take risks in a productive fashion' (p. 64). In the postmodern world described by Giddens social policy must contribute to both individual and societal navigation of risk. Central to this thesis is a change in the balance between security and risk in order actively to produce positive risk takers, so essential to the emerging dynamic entrepreneurial societies envisaged by Giddens (1998b: 100). The present failure of the welfare state to cover risks adequately has a number of sources. The system itself is predicated upon the pooling of risks, rather than the pooling of resources, resulting in an inherently risk-averse system in which risk avoidance and 'moral hazard' are endemic faults (pp. 114–15). In essence, risks are distributed away rather than actively engaged. At its most debilitating this can result in dependency, with welfare recipients avoiding the risks of moving into the labour market in favour of the security of benefits income. In addition, the welfare system cannot respond to the new risks of postmodernity. As Giddens expresses it, either the 'risks covered don't fit with needs' or the 'wrong groups are protected' (p. 116). The 'safety net' of welfare is then deemed to fail on two counts; that is, dependency is encouraged at the expense of entrepreneurial risk taking, and the system of cover is ill-matched to the risks at issue.

The implications for social policy and welfare provision

While some limitations to Giddens's thesis have been identified (see, for example, Lash 1994; Lupton 1999), it is the case that the 'risk society' has severe implications for social policy and traditional welfare systems. These can be expressed under the following themes.

Confidence and legitimacy

The transformative power of social policy has been under attack from critics of both right and left throughout the 1980s and 1990s (Lavalette and Pratt 1997; Leonard 1997), and the ability of traditional forms of social welfare provision to respond to the new risk agenda is doubted (Giddens 1998b). The underpinning rationale and legitimacy of state-driven welfare provision are contested, particularly on the grounds of exclusion, oppression, cost, failure to provide and 'moral hazard' (Parker 1982).

Appropriate coverage, matching and resourcing

The 'New Right' has mounted a considerable challenge to the efficiency, economy and effectiveness of state welfare provision in which appropriate matching to those 'in legitimate need' and the rational allocation of resources have been central issues (Clarke and Newman 1997). During the 'Thatcher years' the introduction of business principles and the 'market' into the bureaucracies of welfare was seen as the most useful way of achieving appropriate coverage, matching and rationalized resource allocation. For some commentators this approach is flawed on practical as well as ideological grounds, not least in the creation of social exclusion as welfare is retrenched to 'deserving' core groups (Leonard 1997), and the operation of a 'safety net' mentality which contributes to dependency and 'moral hazard' (Giddens 1998b). The failure of market economies of welfare to deal adequately with risks has also been increasingly acknowledged, not least by Peter Lilley, the former Thatcherite social services minister, who stated in 1999 that some groups such as the chronically sick were 'virtually uninsurable' and lacked the income power to purchase private cover. In such situations the market is limited: 'hence the need to pool risks through common taxes paid according to income' (*Guardian* 1999). However, Giddens in his work *The Third Way* (1998b) has interestingly questioned exactly what

KEIGHLEY COLLEGE
LIBRARY

should be pooled – risks or resources – and how such pooling should take place: state, market, mixed economy or partnership, for example.

The balance between security and risk

Giddens (1998b: 100) has expressed this as the tension between meeting need and promoting active risk taking, in essence how to move sections of the population out of the safety net of welfare dependency. In the broader sense this also refers to individual and societal capacity to respond to uncertain future risks. To what extent can we have security and certainty and to what extent must we navigate a world of uncertain future hazards? In specific policy terms this is reflected in the increased use of formalized risk assessment methods and the pursuit of early identification, prediction and prevention to protect us from future risks (Kemshall *et al.* 1997).

Prevention and uncertainty

The risk society is an inherently uncertain society. This presents the individual with key challenges, not least in terms of choices and the successful navigation of risk opportunities and threats. As Beck (1992a) expresses it, individuals are shapers of their own worlds, 'making decisions according to calculations of risk and opportunity' (Petersen 1996: 47). They are also increasingly the site of their own failure if risks are managed badly; it is simply a matter of making the wrong choice. In such a climate risk aversion tends to predominate and precaution and prevention are demanded of public policy-makers (most notably in food or environmental risks, but also in the social care and crime arenas). Where government regulation is seen to be weak or compromised (for example, in the GM debate), pressure groups, media, consumers and citizens will make their views clear (*Equinox* 2000). Running parallel to such demands for protection, social policy is increasingly pursuing approaches to risk which pose the individual as responsible for his or her own risk management; for example, personal choices over risky lifestyles, health choices, insurance and personal conduct which avoids risk (Castel 1991; Petersen 1996). This approach stresses the notion of prevention via techniques of early identification and intervention in order to avoid undesirable risks; an approach epitomized by health promotion campaigns (Petersen 1996). Freeman (1992: 44–5) has argued that a social policy of prevention serves a number of key purposes, in particular the management rather than the elimination of social problems, maintenance of the status quo and protection of vested interest, and the reconstruction of social problems as individual choices and responsibilities. In this way, government itself avoids risk, especially to itself, and displaces it upon the individual, or, as a last resort, upon the mediating professionals within the agencies of social welfare provision:

Preventive policy reflects two dominant concerns on the part of the state: these relate . . . to the security of its subjects, but they also include the security of security . . . that is of the prevailing social and political order and of the place of government and the state within it. This implies that the state will seek to relieve the pressure upon it by displacing responsibility for prevention from the primary to the secondary, that is from the institutional to the individual realm.

(Freeman 1992: 49)

The contention is that social policy is no longer about the alleviation of the needs of the individual or the pursuit of the collective good. Instead, it is about the prevention of risk and the displacement of risk management responsibilities on to the 'entrepreneurial self' who must exercise informed choice and self-care to avoid risks (Castel 1991; Petersen 1996).

Conclusions

This chapter has dealt with two contested concepts, *risk* and *social policy*, and the reader has been encouraged to step back from common-sense understandings of what are essentially problematic and contextual notions. Contemporary understandings of risk have been set within the transformation of modernity to late modernity or postmodernity and the recasting of statistically calculated risk to risk as uncertainty. The risks of the risk society are global, indeterminate and internally produced by the processes of industrialization and modernization itself. Risk society is concerned with the distribution of risks rather than the distribution of wealth, and with the avoidance of harms rather than the pursuit of the collective good. The 'modern' agenda of traditional social policy and welfare provision has been challenged by postmodern structural, economic and cultural developments. The chapters that follow examine the extent to which the postmodern discourse of risk is reflected in the policies and institutional practices of the agencies and actors of contemporary welfare. The areas chosen reflect their topicality in current debates about welfare delivery and the use of social policy; for example, care of the elderly, health care, child protection and mental health. Although they are selective and other areas, such as education or needs-related benefits, could have been included, the areas chosen are unified by the common theme of social care delivery and an underpinning rationale of mitigating need. In this sense, they provide key exemplars for investigating the extent to which risk is replacing need as the key organizing principle in health and the personal social services.[1] However, before we explore these exemplars, the next chapter maps the rise of risk as a key feature of welfare discourse and its current place in contemporary social policy debates.

Note

1 The role of risk in penal policy and criminal justice will be addressed in H. Kemshall, *Understanding Risk in Criminal Justice*, in the Open University's Crime and Justice Series (forthcoming).

Suggestions for further reading

Adams, J. (1995) *Risk*. London: University College London. This is an excellent introduction to the key issues in risk assessment and risk perception. Chapter 2 addresses difficulties in measuring risk and the difference between objective measures of risk and subjective perceptions.

Lupton, D. (1999) *Risk*. London: Routledge. This book provides a thorough review of the differing theoretical approaches to understanding risk in contemporary society.

Key organizing principles of social welfare: from need to risk

Introduction

Alaszewski *et al*. (1998: vii) note that health and social welfare are prey to 'fads and fashions'. Key themes and organizing principles of service delivery come and go. The rise and restructuring of local authority personal social services departments in the 1970s, for example, was informed by a desire to meet client need more adequately (Seebohm 1968). The 1980s 'Thatcher years' saw the rise of quality and managerialism, and the recasting of the client as a consumer (Clarke and Newman 1997; Alaszewski *et al*. 1998). The 1990s saw the rise of user empowerment, protection and risk (Kemshall and Pritchard 1996, 1997; Parsloe 1999). Drawing upon an extensive research base Alaszewski *et al*. (1998) have mapped the growing role of risk in health care provision, particularly provision for those labelled as 'vulnerable'. Kemshall *et al*. (1997) have argued that risk has become the dominant *raison d'être* of the personal social services, central to priority setting and rationing, and exhibited in the activities of staff and the managerial systems used to hold them to account. Heyman (1998) has noted the growing preoccupation with risk in health care, due in large part to organizational fears of litigation and economic pressure to ration health care resources. So what has led to the adoption of this risk terminology? To what extent does it mark real changes in social policy and welfare provision? Is it merely the product of 'fashion' or is it the result of more significant changes? Kemshall *et al*. (1997), for example, argue that risk principles are now significantly embedded in the organizational practices of welfare agencies and that the rationale of welfare delivery is predicated increasingly upon risk rather than need. This is exemplified in organizational policies and procedures for service delivery, and in the identification of priorities and resource allocation. The 'risk principle' is evident in worker practices, roles and responsibilities, and in the organization and delivery of key tasks. Thus the substantive changes in policies, procedures and the actual practices of welfare delivery identified by Kemshall *et al.* suggest a radical shift in the rationale of welfare itself. This chapter explores the circumstances and features of this shift from need to risk in more detail.

The rationale of welfare

On a broader front, the legitimacy and rationale of state welfare provision has been questioned (Parker 1982; Murray 1990). In particular, the rationale of need as a key underpinning principle has itself come into question (Jordan 1998). During the 'Thatcher years' the New Right questioned this principle on both economic and ideological grounds. The 'burgeoning cost of welfare' was seen as unsustainable in the long term and hazardous to private wealth creation (Clarke and Newman 1997). This resulted not only in the introduction of market principles into the welfare system, but also in a reappraisal of the concept of need. Two key features of this reappraisal can be discerned: the commodification of welfare and the costing of need; and the redefinition of need in order to exclude sections of the population from provision.

The commodification of welfare

A number of social policy commentators attribute the 'commodification of welfare' to the New Right restructuring of welfare that took place in the 1980s in Britain and the USA (Deakin 1987; Clarke and Newman 1997; Mooney 1997; Pratt 1997). In particular, the introduction of market principles, business practices and notions of consumerism, quality and management has contributed to the redefinition of welfare provision as *product* rather than service. Hugman (1998) has argued that the recasting of welfare as industrial production has its roots in evaluative research into the care of older people, identified as an acute problem in the 1980s as need was projected to rise and resources were limited. The key issues were 'value for money' and efficiency, and the approach quickly spread to other areas of social care provision. The Personal Social Services Research Unit responsible for much of the research defined efficiency as 'a measure of whether society obtained the greatest success in achieving the objectives of welfare programmes (effectiveness) at the least possible cost (economy)' (Hugman 1998: 85). Hugman points out that this approach was adopted by a number of Western countries concerned about welfare spending, including countries such as those in Scandinavia that have a strong ideological and financial commitment to public welfare. He attributes the development of a market economy of welfare in developed countries to three 'underlying factors' (p. 87):

- The loss of legitimacy for publicly funded welfare, not least on the grounds of oppression and injustice, coupled with a mismatch to those 'in need'. The persistence of inequalities paralleled by increasing benefits to the middle class has fuelled this perception.
- Fears of spiralling welfare costs, particularly in respect of ageing populations. This is what Deakin (1987: 119) has referred to as 'pricking the welfare balloons', epitomized by Margaret Thatcher's statement that 'even the Good Samaritan had to have the money to help, otherwise he too would have had to pass on the other side' (quoted in Wapshott and Brock 1983: 278).
- The increasing evidence and perception from the late 1970s onwards of the inefficiency of large scale public services and the low impact of such provision on both need and inequality.

Hugman argues that these factors are interrelated, and that taken together they have formed a forceful rationale for the reconstitution of public welfare as a market, and welfare provision as a product rather than a service. This reframing from service to product in effect changes judgements of welfare from essentially moral ones (i.e. it is morally right to provide the service) to economic ones. The latter involve utilitarian judgements of purpose (what it is for, what it contributes to), and cost–benefit analyses about how this is provided (how much it costs and whether the benefits outweigh the costs). In essence, while welfare service may have been judged in terms of the moral good, the product of welfare is judged in terms of the economic good. In the latter approach, value and utility are measured in terms of price and outcome, not in terms of social justice or moral purpose.

This commodification has been particularly acute in the personal social services, health and more recently probation. In each arena economic efficiency and effectiveness of outcomes have become essential benchmarks, and the late 1980s and 1990s saw the growing adoption of production terminology among senior managers and the rise of what Clarke and Newman (1997) have called the 'New Managerialism'. This period also saw the application of numerous business models to the public sector: from quasi-markets in health, to privatization in some aspects of social care (especially residential care), to the 'pursuit of excellence' and 'total quality management' models in those areas, such as criminal justice, which largely remained outside the market (Peters and Waterman 1982, Morgan and Murgatroyd 1994). However, as Hugman (1998: 92) points out, this restructuring has not been enough to save the welfare state from continued attack: 'Put simply, the debates are still centred around the scale of resources to be allocated to social welfare provision, and the forms of organization desired to deliver such services.' While we may know better what welfare costs, the question of its legitimacy and rationale is still a matter of debate.

Redefining need and exclusion from welfare

Commodification has resulted in a greater preoccupation with unit cost, targeting the most appropriate service at those most in need, an indirect role for the state in much provision and, where users cannot pay the direct costs of privatized provision, services reduced to a minimum safety net by 'responsible' government (Hugman 1998: 93). A further outcome of this economic approach to welfare is the reframing of need from social causes and collective responsibility to individual failings and individual responsibility (Barry 1990: 90). This individualization of need, and of its causes and resolution, legitimates state withdrawal of services from certain users, and assists in the delegitimation of certain needs. Dependent and unproductive citizens are then recast as feckless 'scroungers' responsible for their own fate (Clarke 1996). Such notions have gained both moral and intellectual weight through the concept of 'moral hazard' (Parker 1982; Giddens 1998b), which presumes that the safety net of welfare benefits will produce 'perverse incentives'. That is, the very situations and behaviours insured against will be encouraged by the insurance or benefits system itself: people change their behaviours, become dependent or commit fraud.

Notions of 'genuine need' and of the 'deserving' and 'undeserving' poor are not new; nor is the concept of targeting. The Victorian 'Poor Laws' are an example of the individualization of need and of targeting, and are characteristic of pre-Beveridge approaches to need. However, as Jordan illustrates, this characterization of need was superseded by the post-Second World War welfare state, in which 'universal benefits and services were supposed to meet basic needs that were common to all members of the political community' (Jordan 1998: 100). The key objectives of Beveridge's welfare state were 'The pooling of risks, to protect everyone from shared vulnerability to the contingencies of industrial society, and to establish common standards in the provision for universal needs' (Jordan 1998: 100; see also Beveridge 1942). This formed the underlying principle of the social insurance approach to social policy and welfare typical of the post-Second World War era. The key assumption of such an approach was the expectation that the universal provision of health and education would improve both the individual and collective good, and remove the necessity for selective, means-tested benefits such as income support. The intention was that the safety net of selective benefits would shrink during an age of planned social improvement. As Jordan points out, this has not occurred. Selective benefits have gradually increased, resulting in a growing governmental preoccupation with targeting. Targeting is, of course, as much about who is excluded from welfare provision as it is about who is included. Jordan illustrates this pursuit of 'genuine need' (Blair 1998a) with reference to the reduction in provision to lone parents and the disabled. As Powell (2000) expresses it, New Labour has sought to distinguish between 'good' and 'bad' spending. Spending on education and health is viewed as 'investment', while the social security budget is seen as 'bad', a failure of economic and social policy – in effect, spending on people who 'should be at work' (Blair in Powell 1999).

However, current policy responses to this issue are not mere throwbacks to the pre-Beveridge era. Giddens argues that the risk society entails 'profound changes affecting local life and global order' (Giddens 1998a: 30), not least in terms of responding to internally manufactured risks and the demands of globalization. He characterizes the welfare state, and in particular the National Health Service, as a response to external, natural risks, formulated at a time when risks and traditions could still be taken for granted:

> This is obvious, for example, in the gender provisions in the post 1945 welfare state, which simply presumed the continuity of the 'traditional family'. It is obvious in terms of the growth of the National Health Service, which was set up as a response mechanism to illness understood as external risk.
>
> (Giddens 1998a: 32)

For Giddens the 'risk society' is a far cry from the pre-Beveridge era, and the political and social responses required are radically different. The significant difference is the impact of late modernity and the risk society itself – in particular the impact upon traditional networks, the development of post-Fordist labour markets and forms of production, societal anxieties and responses to manufactured risks, and public scepticism of authority and political legitimacy. Social policy debates and the proposed reconstruction of the welfare state can be placed within this broader context of late modernity.

In *The Third Way* Giddens (1998b: 113) notes that despite the economic challenges made to welfare during the 'Thatcher years', 'the difficulties of the welfare state are only partly financial' and spending has stabilized. For Giddens the problem is one of legitimacy and flexibility. Legitimacy is undermined as the 'wrong people' have their needs met, and as conditions of 'moral hazard' are inadvertently created. Flexibility is inhibited by the bureaucratic nature of the institutions of welfare, and 'institutional stasis' to changing social conditions sets in. For Giddens these are two fundamental reasons to restructure the welfare state away from traditional social insurance mechanisms to meet need, to entrepreneurial, risk-taking activities which stress 'positive welfare' and 'investment in human capital' (Giddens 1998b: 116–17). His proposals are extensively discussed in *The Third Way*, but in essence they contain redefinitions of both need and welfare provision.

Need is recast as social exclusion and inequality, and posed as dysfunctional to both wealth creation and social democracy. Meeting need through economic maintenance (for example, through Income Support) is seen as less socially and politically desirable than promoting greater social inclusion via the labour market. The latter is viewed as more likely to provide people with opportunities to engage in civil life as fully productive citizens. Economic maintenance, no matter how well targeted, is also seen as less economically efficient in the long term due to the disincentives to risk taking and entrepreneurship now required of labour forces by global economies. The welfare system itself is seen as a barrier to flexible responses: 'A high rate of business formation and dissolution is characteristic of a dynamic economy. This flux is not compatible with a society where taken-for-granted habits dominate, including those generated by welfare systems' (Giddens 1998b: 100). In effect, the security traditionally offered by the welfare state, particularly its 'safety net' support offered at times of unemployment, is a disincentive to flexible labour markets in a global economy. Giddens's advice on this point is stark:

> Social democrats have to shift the relationship between *risk* and *security* involved in the welfare state, to develop a society of 'responsible risk takers' in the spheres of government, business enterprise and labour markets. People need protection when things go wrong, but also the material and moral capabilities to move through major periods of transition in their lives.
>
> (Giddens 1998b: 100)

The consequences for the individuals involved may be far from academic. The sale of Rover by the global carmaker BMW in the spring of 2000 illustrated the impact of global markets on national and local economies, and the manner in which large workforces can literally become dispensable overnight. Periods of 'transition' are very real, often with long-term consequences that neither governments nor markets are able to respond to adequately. Such transitions can arise from global and structural changes far removed from the individuals who suffer their consequences, and beyond their abilities to control or influence. In this climate, life can seem very precarious and insecurities abound, not least economic ones. However, Giddens offers us this as a fact of life in late modernity and challenges our traditional expectations that the state will and should protect us from them. In this world the role of the state is reconceptualized, away from the *retrospective* amelioration of individual needs arising from structural inequalities, to the *prospective* distribution of opportunities and chances for inclusion. Simply put, a move away from the redistribution of wealth 'after the event' to the positive creation of future opportunities to obtain wealth (Giddens 1998b: 100–1). The former focuses attention on the assessment and amelioration of need, the latter upon risk-taking opportunities and the ability to live constructively with risk and insecurity. 'New Labour' policies seeking to 'encourage' the disabled and lone parents off benefit and back into the workforce exemplify this type of thinking (Blair 1998a, b; Jordan 1998: 100). Jordan argued that the 'Blair–Clinton' orthodoxy was substantially shifting the discourse of need from the moral and social arenas to the labour market arena:

By emphasing the obligations that accompany rights, and linking these to work contributions, it justifies a kind of equality of opportunity that is formal rather than substantive. It also insists that most needs of the working-age population must be met from earnings in the labour market, and that private provision should replace some of the collective benefits and services that were given as social rights in welfare states.

(Jordan 1998: 103)

This resulted not only in targeting and exclusion from welfare of many traditional welfare beneficiaries, but also in the erosion of any residual legitimacy left for the concept of 'deserving poor' and need. Jordan identified the core political constituency of the Blair–Clinton orthodoxy as those with the most to fear from global economic forces, and whose economic future are most prey to global markets and technological change. These groups were appealed to on two grounds: the first that they have assumed too high a proportion of the tax burden, and the second that such taxes have been redistributed to those barely less well off than themselves and to those reluctant to enter the workforce. As Jordan put it, 'no wonder they can be mobilized in favour of radical reforms of welfare benefits and services, and have little sympathy with those who look like free-riders, cheats or opportunists, and far less deserving than themselves' (Jordan 1998: 105). There is, however, a cost attached to such populism (Jordan 1998). The excluded are deemed to be excluded by their own design, their own inadequacy to respond appropriately to risks and insecurities; excluded because of personal mismanagement or by desire. In this climate the legitimacy and rationale for even 'safety net' benefits is eroded and needs are reduced to issues of personal mismanagement or miscalculation of risks which should have been foreseen and avoided (O'Malley 1992, 1996).

Summary

This section has argued that the recent social policy and welfare preoccupation with risk is more than just 'fashion'. Its roots lie within the 1980s reframing of public welfare as a market and the commodification of welfare as a costed product. This 'restructuring' of welfare provision within a largely economic discourse has also resulted in a relocation of need to individual failings and away from the social sphere, paralleled by a growing delegitimization of even residual needs. The 'Third Way' emphasis upon labour market rather than welfare solutions to inequality and social exclusion, epitomized by the 'Blair–Clinton orthodoxy', has also challenged traditional social insurance responses to need. Risk and insecurity are increasingly replacing the concepts of need and security in welfare provision. The post-1945 social policy agenda of social insurance and 'after the event' compensation for social inequalities has been challenged as economically inefficient and ineffective in promoting social inclusion. Notions of social investment, the promotion of human capital and flexibility in the face of insecurity and risk are now advocated as key ingredients of Giddens's positive welfare. Social policy is no longer solely about the reduction and alleviation of external risks; it is also about the promotion of active responses to the internal and global risks of the 'risk society'. The next section examines this reframing of current social policy in more detail.

Social investment and the promotion of risk taking

The 'Thatcher years' and the programme of the 'New Right' eroded the notion of social insurance and in many respects reconfigured needs as the result of personal misfortune and the failure to risk manage appropriately (Rose 1996). Citizens were expected to take out private insurance against many of the previously constituted collective risks, such as old age, ill-health and unemployment (Association of British Insurers 1995). Such hazards were reconstituted as a fact of late modern life, against which the prudent citizen should take the most appropriate action. In addition to the obvious forms of private insurance, this could also include: retraining to update and transfer skills to more productive parts of the labour market; geographical mobility (literally 'on yer bike') to follow emergent industries such as computing; and an active commitment to education and 'life-long learning' to remain flexible and productive in the workforce. As Rose expresses it, such *prudentialism* requires the citizen to adopt a calculating attitude towards almost all his or her decisions, whether these be the traditional risks of the welfare state, or decisions over healthy eating choices or the installation of burglar alarms. Thus the individual becomes the primary site of risk management, not society, and the 'good' citizen is the responsible, prudential one.

Prudence is of course not a new concept. The Victorian age stressed prudential behaviour along with its emphasis upon the 'deserving poor'. However, Rose (1996: 60) contends that what *is* new here is the 'construction of active citizenship in an active society', and that this underpins contemporary governmental forms regardless of political spectrum or political ideology. For Rose this is the hallmark of 'advanced liberal' societies in which the technique of government is through the promotion of individual responsibility. Like Jordan he sees the dangers for the excluded:

> Those 'excluded' from the benefits of a life of choice and self-fulfilling aspirations have been deformed by the dependency culture, whose efforts at self-advancement have been frustrated for so long that they suffer from 'learned helplessness', whose self-esteem has been destroyed . . . they are to be assisted . . . through their engagement in a whole array

of programmes for their ethical reconstruction as active citizens – training to equip them with skills of self-promotion, counselling to restore their self-worth and self-esteem, programmes of empowerment to enable them to assume their rightful place as the self-actualising and demanding subjects of an 'advanced' liberal democracy.

(Rose 1996: 60)

The new politics of welfare: the 'Third Way'

In Britain and the USA one outcome of the 'market-minded radicalism' of the Thatcher–Reagan years has been 'high unemployment and polarisation leading to social division and political conflict' (Jordan 1998: 11). Concerns with social exclusion and an 'underclass' (Murray 1989) began to dominate much of the late 1990s social policy agenda, particularly in the USA and Britain (Blair 1998b), and how to respond to those citizens who failed to become 'self-actualizing' was a key issue. The rapid spread and impact of a global economy exacerbated this problem, as traditional markets and forms of production were displaced, and First World economies found their traditional economic primacy challenged by emerging economies and transnational markets (Burrows and Loader 1994; Giddens 1998b; Jordan 1998). The 'new politics of welfare' seeks to manage the impact of these significant changes upon labour, particularly traditional forms of labour trapped by educational or geographical immobility. However, as Jordan notes, this is not through the identification and alleviation of individual need as a moral right, but through the 'Third Way' programme of social investment and opportunity creation:

> It emphasizes equality of opportunity rather than outcome, and rights to education and training rather than benefits. It wants meritocratic access to positions of power and economic advantage, and it allows the rewards for these to be more unequal than in the regimes for social justice in the 1970s. And it provides for 'genuine' needs to be met, with far stricter testing for the authenticity of the claims from unemployment and disability.
>
> (Jordan 1998: 18)

The 'Third Way' as a label is not the preserve of any one politician or any one social theorist. However, it is increasingly associated with 'New Labour' and Blair (Blair and Schroeder 1999), and with the reconstruction of social democracy advocated by Giddens. For Giddens (1998b: 26) the 'Third Way' 'refers to a framework of thinking and policy-making that seeks to adapt social democracy to a world which has changed fundamentally over the past two or three decades' and which seeks to 'transcend both old style social democracy and neoliberalism'. The following key strands can be identified in the Third Way although the extent to which they are fully embedded in the Blairite programme varies:[1]

- social justice (including social inclusion and equality);
- social responsibility and obligations;
- the labour market as a mechanism for achieving social justice;
- reward for merit and an emphasis upon meritocracy;
- alleviation of need confined to residual, 'appropriately targeted' and 'genuine need';
- modernization.

Social justice

Social justice can be defined as a redistributive, reformist programme with its roots in liberalism (Giddens 1998b). In essence it is concerned to ameliorate the worst excesses of capitalism and to increase every citizen's access to economic rewards. Capitalism remains unchallenged, economic efficiency is promoted as a public good and social justice is ensured by greater access to the labour market and its rewards, coupled with an increased emphasis upon meritocracy. Inequality is reconfigured as social exclusion from education, the labour market and the wealth creation opportunities these afford. As such, inequality is tackled by programmes of social inclusion, including those with elements of compulsion (like 'workfare' programmes) and greater equality of opportunity and access. State funds are redirected towards key elements of the social and economic infrastructure like education and skill development, and away from the alleviation of individual misfortune. Social investment in human capital is seen as central to national regeneration and economic growth, with attendant benefits for all.

Social responsibility and obligation

The commitment to social justice also carries with it a moral imperative which stresses civic obligations and responsibilities, epitomized in the government's catch-phrase that there are 'no rights without responsibilities'. As Jordan (1998: 42) expresses it,

> The redefinition of social justice in the new orthodoxy focuses on the need to create a 'something for something society' in which 'rights are matched by responsibilities.' The principle of reciprocity states that those who enjoy the economic benefits of social cooperation have a corresponding obligation to make a productive contribution to that community . . . It emphasizes the injustice of 'free-riding' on the efforts of others, and the requirement of institutional arrangements for social justice to forbid the exploitation of the hard-working by the idle that is allowed by unconditional benefits.

Reciprocity and mutual obligation are cast as both moral and economic concepts, essential for the public good and civil society, and for economic prosperity. The exclusionary implications for those who *will not* contribute are clear. Their rights and benefits are eroded. They are in effect redesignated as non-deserving 'non-contributors', and can be subject to compulsory mechanisms to make them contribute, or to legal redress for their 'free-loading'; for example, the 'tough new measures' announced on 5 April 2000 to deal with the benefit fraud committed by the estimated 1 million people working in the 'black economy' and also claiming Social Security benefits. The Employment Secretary announced that it was a 'move from the welfare state to the working state' (*PM*, BBC Radio 4). On the other hand, those who *cannot* contribute are subjected to greater scrutiny and stricter tests of their incapacity; for example, lone parents and the disabled. While Third Way politics stresses that such obligations apply to all, in practice they have tended to be most applied to welfare recipients, and the obligations of 'big business' are less frequently emphasized (Powell 2000).

Social justice via the labour market

Following his election to office Tony Blair (1997) promised to 'put the work ethic at the centre of the welfare state'. The work ethic is seen as central to economic prosperity and national regeneration, in addition to carrying a moral benefit for the individuals involved and for society as a whole. It also marks a social policy shift from the retrospective alleviation of need through benefits, to a prospective system of incentives to work such as tax credits and family working credits to assist the low paid. The labour market is seen as the key arena for removing dependency and enhancing participation in civil life. Social engineering through the creation and uptake of opportunities is seen as the key to relieving social ills such as the 'dependency culture', the existence of an 'underclass', poverty and social exclusion. Social investment in education, life-long learning, new technologies and skill development are seen as more efficient mechanisms to achieve these ends than the maintenance of universal state benefits to meet need.

The promotion of a meritocracy

The work ethic and the notion of the socially responsible, productive citizen are used to justify differential rewards within a system which prioritizes social justice. In effect, those who contribute the most should receive the most. Opportunity should also be governed by merit, so access to 'position', whether in public or business life, should be a matter of merit, although in principle such opportunities are open to all. The unproductive are deemed to be without merit unless they adapt their behaviours to service the economic good and become self-actualizing citizens. In this climate, claims based on need are superseded by claims based on merit. What one can do, and what one can offer, become more important than what one cannot.

Residual and targeted need

Need and the universal claim to have 'basic needs' addressed were the key principles of the Beveridge welfare state (Beveridge 1942). However, this approach has been brought into disrepute, not least through arguments about 'dependency' and 'moral hazard', inappropriate targeting of need and the failure of the welfare state to achieve wholesale redistribution of wealth and goods. The labour market is now posed as the key mechanism of redistribution and needs will be met through the provision of opportunities to work. Those who 'genuinely' cannot enter the workforce are treated as a special residual category for whom special measures will be implemented (e.g. counselling and support *into* employment), or for whom benefits will be paid if strict eligibility criteria are met. As stated above, the potential for this 'genuine' category to shrink is great, and the legitimacy for even 'safety net' needs to be met has been eroded.

Modernization

Modernization is also seen as central to national regeneration and future economic prosperity. Flexible, highly skilled and adaptable workforces are seen as essential to competitiveness in the global market. Traditional, displaced workforces from older manufacturing industries cannot presume any greater protection under New Labour than they enjoyed during the Thatcher years. Indeed, they may enjoy less as they are encouraged to modernize, adapt and learn new skills. Safety nets themselves are seen as barriers to flexible responses in the post-Fordist labour market. Flexibility is promoted through the active embracement of new technologies, constant updating through 'lifelong learning' and the notion of portable skills. Competence is upgraded to a higher plane, from mere competence on the job, to 'meta-competence' or learning to learn (Kemshall 2000). The 'modernizing agenda' has been particularly acute in public sector welfare organizations – for example, health and social care – and in criminal justice. In particular, the notion of incremental public spending has been replaced by a notion of rational public spending (Blair and Schroeder 1999) in which inputs and outputs are tightly linked. The Comprehensive Spending Review proposed in the White Paper *Modern Public Services for Britain* (July 1998) not only proposed more spending on 'good welfare' but also linked expenditure to reform of public services and modernization. Key themes were the increase in departmental accountability to the Treasury, and more direct expenditure at the frontline and less on bureaucracy, accompanied by the avoidance of duplication and the advocacy of 'joined up government'.

Modernization has been paralleled by an increased emphasis upon pragmatism rather than ideology in the framing of social policy. For New Labour 'what counts is what works', and the recycling of Conservative policies which appear to have utility is viewed as entirely acceptable (Labour Party 1997). This has resulted in a somewhat eclectic and pragmatic approach to policy (Powell 2000), in which utility outweighs ideology.

The impact of the Third Way

The Third Way is not without its critics: from those who doubt the contribution of third way policies to flexible, post-Fordist production (Pierson 1994, 1998); to those who wish to promote a more 'emancipatory' agenda towards postmodern welfare (Leonard 1997); or those like Jordan (1998) who foresee a diminished role for national social policies in the face of global capital and global markets. Space precludes a critical review here.[2] However, what is of significance is the Third Way conception of social policy and its connections to the risk society. Giddens offers the Third Way as the preferred means of assisting citizens to 'pilot their way through the major revolutions of our time: globalisation, transformations in personal life and our relationship to nature' (Giddens 1998b: 64). These 'major revolutions' are expressed as the five interrelated dilemmas of the risk society:

- Globalization – of economies and markets as well as of risks. Economic globalization and its attendant technological changes are seen as eroding nation states and the closed systems of single economies. Most markets and most technologies are now transnational.
- Individualization – expressed primarily as the demise of traditional solidarities and social forms such as family and class. As collective identities are weakened, the world is experienced and negotiated individually. The security offered by traditional life-courses is diminished, and the individual is confronted by myriad choices with little guidance on how to choose. Hence the lived experience of the individual is one of greater insecurity.
- The demise of 'left–right' politics in which traditional party ideologies have less impact than social democratic 'centre radicalism'; hence political formulations like 'New Labour' and the promotion of advanced liberalism as a political philosophy (Rose 1996).
- Challenges to political agency and the demise of democracy, expressed as lack of trust in politicians and apathy about formal political systems, paralleled by an increase in 'sub-politics' through activist and single issue groups like Greenpeace (Beck 1992a). Increasingly the political arena is outside formal democratic structures like parliaments, and in pressure groups and consumer organizations that seek to control and influence global corporations in ways that individual governments cannot (Greenpeace upon Shell over the Brent Spar oil rig disposal for example).

- Ecological issues and environmental concerns – the recognition that modernity is the site of risk and that 'Coping with ecological risk will be a problematic for the foreseeable future' (Giddens 1998b: 60). This is not just a matter of managing ecological threats. It is also a matter of how risk is approached and managed. For Giddens this is not entirely a matter of defensive action and risk avoidance. While the 'precautionary principle' is seen to have its place in the face of incalculable and unforeseeable risks, risk is not viewed as an entirely negative construct. Risks require active assessment and management, and risk-taking activities, such as those that contribute to the public good, are positively encouraged. The lessons for the social realm are also drawn: 'Who should bear responsibility for the future consequences of present activities (whether of individuals, nations or other groups) is one of the major concerns of the new politics, as is who provides security if things go wrong, how and with what resources. Opportunity and innovation are the positive side of risk. No one can escape risk . . . but there is a basic difference between the passive experience of risk and the active exploration of risk environments. A positive engagement with risk is a necessary component of social and economic mobilization . . . We all need protection against risk, but also the capability to confront and take risks in a productive fashion' (Giddens 1998b: 63–4).

In welfare terms this has resulted in a 'redrawing of the boundaries between the individual and the state' (Powell 2000: 56) and the emergence of 'DIY welfare' (Klein and Millar 1995), in which individuals are increasingly responsible for their risks. The significance of the Third Way is its recognition that risk is central to late modern life, and that both political forms and social policy should actively engage with the risk society.

Summary

The notion of social insurance, and the concept of state alleviation of individual need central to it, has been replaced by social justice and the concept of the active, responsible and prudential citizen. Social policy reform and programmes of redistribution are now pursued through the labour market and the social engineering of 'opportunities' to contribute (for example, through education and workfare). Social investment in human capital is viewed as more economically productive and efficient than the retrospective alleviation of individual need through a state benefit system. Categories of residual need are gradually reduced, and replaced by the promotion of social obligation and economic contribution. The dependency of need and the 'need culture' is seen as a barrier to economic flexibility and national responsiveness to global markets. A social policy (the 'Third Way') which actively promotes risk taking and a positive attitude to risks has gained currency, and is advocated as the most effective response to the dilemmas of the 'risk society'.

Conclusions: is it all risk and no need?

Is the move from a needs-based welfare system to a risk-based social invest-ment system a change of focus or a radical shift? Contemporary discussions of targeting and 'genuine need' would suggest that a needs-based discourse still remains at the heart of current social policy and welfare systems, and the issue remains the traditional one of more accurately identifying and responding to need (Bradshaw 1972, 1994). Other commentators have noted the presence of risk concerns in traditional welfarism, and have characterized the Beveridge welfare state as a social insurance system against a multitude of risks that may befall the individual (Simon 1987; Giddens 1998b). How distinct, then, are *need* and *risk*, and how are these apparent contradictions in analyses of social policy and welfare provision to be understood?

The changes in the rationale of welfare outlined in this chapter illustrate that need has played a varied role in the construction and delivery of welfare, and has been subject to numerous changes since the inception of the post-war welfare state. While a 'needs-based' discourse has always underpinned wel-fare, this discourse has in practice been subject to numerous social, economic and political processes in its construction and use (Langan 1998), and has often operated alongside concerns with risks; for example, protection from the external risks of disease, accidental injury and unemployment (Simon 1987). Beveridge originally conceived of the welfare state as a safety net system to guarantee a minimum level of income for those who fell out of the workforce through no fault of their own. As Langan (1998: 8) impor-tantly reminds us, this was not done to alleviate individual need for its own sake, but was pursued as part of the larger mission to 'promote the reconstruction of a new social order' in post-war Britain. The original welfare state importantly embedded notions of risk and insurance responses to individual and collective risks within its founding principles through concepts like National Insurance and income maintenance, although, as noted above, these risks were always understood as externally located. Key mechanisms of delivery, particularly through the large bureaucratic agencies like health and the personal social services, also reflected an insurance approach to needs assessment and delivery, through group categorizations (such as 'the disabled' and 'the elderly') and by delivering to whole sections of the population regardless of individual need (free school milk to all pupils, for example: Langan 1998).

While the mechanisms of delivery may have had features of actuarial risk underpinning them, at its inception the welfare state reflected a social policy in which *social* rather than *individual* risk was guarded against, and needs were framed as universal, basic and no fault (Doyal and Gough 1991; Percy-Smith 1996). The early years of the welfare state were characterized by a belief that need could be objectively defined, clearly identified and resourced according to strict hierarchical priorities (Glennerster 1983). The initial welfare state was underpinned by three principles:

- Universalism – that is, all welfare services were available free at point of delivery to everyone according to their need.
- Social citizenship – that is, a desire to promote a sense of belonging and good order in the newly reconstructed post-war Britain.
- Paternalism – that is, needs were defined and met by the benevolent state (Langan 1998: 8–10).

During this period need was framed as objective, measurable and universal, although in the practical delivery of welfare services need was heavily defined by central policy-makers, experts and professionals (Langan 1998). By the 1970s the concept of need and the notion of universal entitlement were under challenge. Economists, in particular, challenged the notion of objective need existing outside the market arena of wants or preferences, and the value-laden nature of defining need was recognized (Percy-Smith 1996). Bradshaw (1972) attempted to deal with this difficulty through a 'taxonomy of need' which proved to have a number of flaws, not least the tension between the normative definition of need framed by policy-makers and experts, and the felt or expressed need of citizens (Kemshall 1984). This tension was exacerbated by subjecting need to an economic discourse in which universalism and the benevolent state were severely challenged. The economic discourse of need introduced two important precursors of a more overtly risk discourse: individualized need as personal misfortune and the notion of the prudential citizen.

The location of need within economic discourse throughout the 1970s and 1980s, especially during the 'New Right' period, saw the language of need increasingly replaced by the language of priorities. As Bradshaw (1994: 47) puts it, 'the questions are not what need is and who is in need but who is to have first claim on limited resources and who is to judge that claim? What are the trade-offs?' (Bradshaw 1994: 47). During the 'Thatcher years' this became not just a question of economic priorities but also a question of legitimacy, particularly given the persistence of inequality and the rising cost of welfare. Who should be included in the welfare net and who should not became the key issue, and notions of selective need rather than universal need gained currency. The balance between public and private provision was also radically altered (Langan 1998). The prudential citizen was increasingly targeted by private insurance offering security against the risks of unemployment, ill-health and old age (Association of British Insurers 1995) to replace the diminished state provision against what had been seen as collective needs. By the arrival of New Labour in the mid-1990s the acceptance of rationing was commonplace and the principle of targeted or 'selective' need rather than universal need was central to most welfare provision (Langan 1998). Langan argues that welfare provision in the late 1990s can be characterized as 'needs-led' welfare, and she discerns a growing political consensus around the principle of selective welfare provision based upon individual (rather than basic or universal) need. However, who these individuals are and what power they have to assert their needs in the face of limited resources and organizational definitions of their need is a moot point. Health treatment according to post code and difficulties in exercising parental choice of schools are just two examples. Langan notes that the 'elevation of responsibility over rights, of individualism over collectivism, and of community over class' (p. 27) has diminished traditional needs, and with them the traditional welfare constituency of the lone parents, the disabled, the impoverished, the unemployed, the young, the excluded and the elderly. Individuals actually have less power to assert their needs, and the 'residualizing' of welfare noted above is one outcome of needs-led welfare.

By the late 1990s the issue was no longer how to target need more appropriately. Instead, the issue was one of 'tackling social exclusion' through the targeted use of social inclusion programmes and the strategic use of the labour market. Needs-led welfare was transformed into the risk-led, positive welfare of the Third Way. This transformation is presented in Table 2.1.

Aharoni (1981) described the welfare state as a 'no-risk society' in which welfarism promised security from myriad external risks. The social engineering of welfarist social policy directed at such risks and the personal needs and hardships they cause was generally accepted. The citizen was seen as a 'no-fault' victim of such hazards. Risk-led social policy accepts risk as a fact of late modern life, a source of opportunity as well as threat, 'an avenue for enterprise and the creation of wealth, and thus an unavoidable and invaluable part of the progressive environment' (O'Malley 1996: 204). Protection is afforded to the citizen in only the most specific of cases, residualist responses are the order of the day and prudential and self-actualizing citizenry is encouraged. The principle of social engineering in 'advanced liberal' social policy is one of residual state care, encouragement of individual

Table 2.1   Welfare society to risk society

Welfare society	Risk society
Universal welfare	Residual welfare
Risk protection	Risk promotion
Social insurance	Social justice
'No fault' exposure to risk	The 'prudential' citizen

risk management as social responsibility and obligation, and reduction of personal hardship and attendant needs through the labour market. State responsibility for risk management is thus reduced, although conversely this lack of mediation of personal risk by the state promotes personal and thereby collective flexibility and responsivity to risk. In the absence of 'safety nets', risk nettles do have to be grasped.

Notes

1 While the Blair programme is usually discussed as part of the dual Blair–Clinton orthodoxy, the discussion here is confined to British social policy, as the book's focus is risk, social policy and welfare in Britain.
2 Jordan (1998) provides an excellent critique.

Suggestions for further reading

Burrows, R. and Loader, B. (1994) *Towards a Post-Fordist Welfare State?* London: Routledge. This is an accessible and comprehensive edited work on the post-Fordist restructuring of the welfare state.
Giddens, A. (1998) *The Third Way.* Cambridge: Polity Press. This is the seminal work presenting Giddens's position on the 'Third Way'.
Giddens, A. (1999) *Runaway World: How Globalisation is Reshaping Our Lives.* London: Profile Books. This book presents Giddens's Reith Lectures on the 'Runaway World', and presents his views on the 'risk society', globalization and the transition of modernity to late modernity or postmodernity.
Leonard, P. (1997) *Postmodern Welfare: Reconstructing an Emancipatory Project.* London: Sage. This is a difficult but useful exploration of postmodernity and its implications for welfare states.

chapter

three

Health care: the rise of risk, health promotion and rationing

Introduction

Health care provision is viewed by many as the last bastion of the traditional welfare state, much 'tinkered with' but at heart still based upon principles of universal need and available free at point of delivery. As such it presents an excellent arena in which the emerging residualist and risk-led rationale of welfare provision can be tested. In brief, it provides a key test of whether claims to postmodern and post-Fordist welfare provision are substantiated or over-stated, and whether risk has replaced need. Health care provision has not been immune from radical overhaul and has seen the introduction of markets, a growing 'mixed economy' of provision and increased commodification of provision (for example, through the costing of treatments and restrictions on 'expensive drugs').

The perceived crisis in the National Health Service, exacerbated by annual bed shortages, has fuelled the debate on health care funding (Barkham 2000). How to pay for health care has become a vexed question, with answers ranging from private alternatives (Gladstone 1997), to health insurance models (Association of British Insurers 1995), to notions of stakeholder welfare (Field 1996). The current Blairite response has been a combination of proposals such as:

- 'hypothecated taxes' aimed directly at the NHS (Milburn 2000a);
- restructuring of accident and emergency units and the NHS Direct telephone service aimed at easing waiting lists;
- the abolition of the internal market and the establishment of primary care trusts in the 1999 Health Act.

This has been paralleled by increased spending (Blair 2000a; Elliott *et al.* 2000), although the extent of 'real spend' has been hotly debated (Barkham

2000). However, the transition from universal, centrally funded health care provision to more radical forms has yet to be achieved, and illustrates two key difficulties in the post-Fordist welfare thesis highlighted by Harris and McDonald (2000). The first is the lack of attention to existing institutional arrangements and their mediating effect upon broader macro-social and economic change, and the second is the lack of detailed empirical evidence for a radical shift from modern to postmodern welfare provision (Harris and McDonald 2000: 51–3). Health care provision is a key example of both difficulties.

The 50-year history of the NHS has been one of almost constant change and adaptation as health care has responded to demographic change, rising expectations, technological change and ideological assault (Wall and Owen 1999). Despite such responsiveness, Wall and Owen contend that successive governments have committed themselves to its founding principles of 'universality, comprehensiveness, and equity', and this has ensured the continued existence of state health care provision (p. 148). At the height of the Thatcher years, Margaret Thatcher herself contended that the health service was 'safe in our hands'. More recently, Tony Blair has reasserted government support for the principles of the NHS (Blair 2000a). Throughout its history state health care provision has been the site of both conflict and change, but also of adaptation and mediation. Fundamental questioning of underpinning principles is a relatively recent phenomenon (Wall and Owen 1999) and has been expressed principally through the New Right reliance upon privatization and markets, and more recently through a shift from secondary to primary care (Department of Health 1997). In addition, the National Health Service has long struggled to fulfil its promise of universal access, response to need and improving the nation's health. Purdy and Banks (1999) outline the numerous inequalities of gender, race and class which impact upon people's access to and experience of health care, and the exclusionary practices of the NHS which have persisted irrespective of the government in power. The NHS has a long history of adaptation and change to political, economic and social circumstances, in addition to perennial difficulties in delivering its mandate. What, if anything, is different now?

Risk and developments in health policy

Drawing extensively upon the work of Beck (1992a) and Giddens (1991), Nettleton and Burrows (1998) argue that the increased individualization, reflexivity and risk of late modernity or postmodernity have all impacted upon recent developments in health policy. They argue that in a society increasingly characterized by uncertainty and risk, individuals are 'encouraged to make life-style choices and life-planning decisions' (p. 164). The necessity of such choices is particularly acute as welfare, and in this case state health provision is characterized by retrenchment and residualism. The commodification of welfare and the attendant economic framing of provision recasts the service user as a consumer, both entitled to and required to make choices. While such choice may in reality be heavily constrained by economic resource and social capital (such as education and information access), rationally informed health risk management choices are expected of the individual (Greco 1993; Nettleton 1997).

Information is the 'bed-rock' of such choices: information on hospital performance and league tables, health education and promotion campaigns (on smoking, drinking, healthy eating, for example), and private health care alternatives. Ill-health is increasingly linked to lifestyle (Department of Health 1992; Klein 1995) and as such is seen as a matter of choice. Such choices carry moral weight and responsibility (Greco 1993), a sign of the rational and responsible citizen acting well. This moral imperative is underpinned by the welfare shift from the amelioration of need to the prevention of risk (Giddens 1994: 151–73), and in health care is expressed through policy concerns with disease prevention and health promotion; that is, health risk prevention and management. As Nettleton and Burrows express it, this means a concern with those who are well, as well as with those who are sick, and extends health care beyond the boundaries of the NHS.

Three main strands can be discerned in recent health care policy in which risk plays a key role. These are:

- health promotion;
- insurance and private health care;
- redeployment of state provision from secondary to primary care, coupled with rationing and the questioning of universal provision.

This chapter reviews developments in each of these areas, and concludes by considering the implications of such developments for health care practice and management.

Risk and health promotion

In *The Health of the Nation* (Department of Health 1992) the government outlined its strategy for improving the health of the nation. This document highlighted health risks stemming from lifestyle choices such as alcohol consumption, smoking, diet and exercise, and linked health to twentieth-century manufactured risks. The document foregrounded choice, risk and prevention as central features of health care, and extended the notion of state-driven health policy beyond the confines of the NHS (Klein 1995). For some commentators (Scott and Williams 1991; Klein 1995; Petersen 1997) this represented the culmination of a growing ideological shift in health care policy from 'the notion that the state should protect the health of individuals to the idea that individuals should take responsibility to protect themselves from risk' evident in health care provision from the mid-1970s (Petersen 1997: 194).

Petersen, for example, argues that recent health policy can be understood as a feature of Rose's advanced liberalism (Rose 1993, 1996), discussed in Chapter 2 of this text. What Petersen labels the 'new public health' is characterized by reference to the citizen as a rational agent, the entrepreneurial individual able to make informed, reflexive choices about his or her care (Rose 1993: 288), and consequently the health risks they are choosing to run or avoid. Advanced liberalism requires the individual to self-regulate, and health care is no exception. In this context, health promotion can be seen as a mechanism for re-educating irrational citizens, and for lessening the burden on collective provision by promoting self-care. Petersen contends that while this shift has been subtle, it has been effective, not least because it has: 'served the objective of privatising health by distributing responsibility for managing risk throughout the social body while at the same time creating new possibilities for intervention in private lives' (Petersen 1997: 194).

This broad approach to health care, with its emphasis upon promotion and prevention, has brought new risks within the health care remit: environmental risks, occupational risks, dietary risks and the lifestyle risks of individuals (for example drug use) to name just a few. As Green (1997) has argued, the notion of prevention embodies notions of blameworthiness, poor judgement and lack of calculability about future risks on behalf of the citizen. Other, better choices and courses of action could have been adopted. It is the individual's fault that they were not. Castel (1991) has argued that both prevention and the responsibility for 'self-care' are rooted in an increasingly calculative attitude towards risk: any risky behaviour or event can be foreseen and prevented. As Nettleton (1997: 208) puts it,

> contemporary forms of welfare are increasingly requiring that individuals take personal responsibility for their own future and purchase goods and services which are designed to meet their personal requirements. A range of risks are presented by the 'experts' and it is up to individuals to calculate the likely consequences of certain actions for themselves.

Within recent health promotion and prevention policy this approach is exemplified by the following:

- the production of the 'at-risk' self (Petersen 1997, 1999) and the promotion of self-care and self-regulation (Greco 1993);
- surveillance and regulation of lifestyles (Gordon 1991).

The 'at-risk self' and the promotion of self-care and self-regulation

Health care is no longer the sole preserve of the NHS. Private health care, often supported by various insurance mechanisms, has grown (Association of British Insurers 1995), and the implicit reliance of the state upon informal care in the community has continued (Purdy and Banks 1999). In addition to the increased marketization of health care, there has been an increased emphasis upon conceptualizing health as lying within the individual's control, and on 'active citizens [having] a right and a duty to maintain, contribute to and ensure (or should that be insure?) their health status' (Nettleton 1997: 208). Central to this view is the notion of 'making an informed choice' based upon rational consideration of expert information, and a shift in health care intervention from post-disease treatments to the promotion of healthy lifestyles and the eradication of risky behaviours such as smoking. Recent literature on the 'new public health', as this trend has been dubbed, outlines three main reasons for its development:

- the New Right ideology of the Thatcher years (Purdy and Banks 1999);
- the impact of post-Fordism on welfare provision (Burrows and Loader 1994);
- the rise of advanced liberal modes of governance in postmodern society (Rose 1993, 1996; Petersen 1997).

While there are academic disputes about the extent of each one's impact upon current social policy and welfare provision (Carter 1998), there is evidence that each has played a significant role in constructing the 'at-risk self' as a site of health promotion and risk prevention.

The New Right and health risks

The 1980s saw a crisis of confidence in the state's long-term ability to fund state health care, and a system of radical restructuring to provide a 'mixed economy' of health care provision followed (Purdy and Banks 1999). Formal alternative provision from the private sector was encouraged, coupled with the introduction of market principles into bureaucratic state provision. Affordability and the pursuit of new systems for funding health care became central issues, with suggestions ranging from internal markets, compulsory insurance, targeted health care taxes and privatization, to payment at point of delivery. While the internal market combined with a degree of private provision became the favoured option and more radical options have not been pursued, the mixed economy model has importantly challenged a number of traditional notions of health care delivery. The most significant challenges have been to:

- notions of universal entitlement;
- the state's sole responsibility for health care provision;

- a medical needs-led system of provision;
- hospital-based services;
- a curative responsive health care delivered to the sick.

In essence, critics of the NHS argued that it was a 'sickness service not a health service' (D. Green 1997). From the 1970s onwards policy began to reflect this change of direction from a curative to a preventative service (Wall and Owen 1999), most notably by placing responsibility for prevention upon health authorities (DHSS 1976; Royal Commission 1979). This emphasis continued in the 1980s (DHSS 1981, 1987), and most notably with the Acheson Report in 1988, which emphasized health promotion and healthy lifestyles. This in effect spawned the 'new public health' movement epitomized by the Public Health Alliance, which emphasized that the 'protection of the public and the prevention of illness should be given priority over costly individual intervention' (Wall and Owen 1999).[1] By 1991 the Department of Health was talking of the need 'to focus as much on the promotion of good health and the prevention of disease as on the treatment, care and rehabilitation of those who fall ill' (Department of Health 1991a: vii).

While the moral and economic debate on the future of the NHS continues, the challenge to the traditional notions underpinning collective provision has assisted in facilitating the development of a discourse of health promotion and individual responsibility for health care. Markets imply choice and, along with it, responsibility for such choices. Alternatives imply selection, judgement and calculation over options. Responsibility for health care choices and provision is displaced away from the state, and the monopoly of state hospital care and medical needs is broken by private provision and the costs of the market. The citizen can choose, but in the activation of that choice the citizen also assumes responsibility. The replacement of a medical needs model with a health promotion one is attractive on moral and political grounds as well as economic ones. Economically prevention is more desirable than cure, although the extent of savings (if any) is a matter of considerable debate (Wall and Owen 1999). Targeting is notoriously inefficient, and many costs of health promotion campaigns are hidden. Evaluating the outcomes of such campaigns is also difficult (for example, the costs of cancer breast screening for the numbers saved) and such calculations remain a matter of moral as well as economic judgement. Foster, for example, has challenged the effectiveness of breast screening. Based upon the 26 authorities that had kept figures up to 1989, of the 164,000 women screened only 733 women were subsequently diagnosed with breast cancer (Foster 1995) – in effect a sledge hammer to crack a nut. The debate has continued, with Blanks *et al.* (2000) claiming a real decrease in mortality of 21.3 per cent between 1990 and 1998, of which only 6.4 per cent is attributable to screening, and 14.9 per cent to other factors such as improvements in treatment. However, health promotion can avoid some of the difficult moral and political debates over NHS rationing and the allocation of treatments and drugs. The stark issues of rationing at the point of delivery of treatment can be softened. In addition, those who present with 'self-inflicted risks' derived from unhealthy lifestyles and risky behaviours, such as drug addiction, alcohol misuse and smoking, can be more readily deprioritized for costly treatments if they are deemed to be blameworthy for their own medical condition. Difficult and contentious issues of rationing are therefore circumvented.

Post-Fordist health care

While the definitions of both Fordism and post-Fordism are a matter of debate (Pierson 1994), Fordism is broadly defined as the period between the Second World War and the 1970s and is characterized by economic growth, mass production, free markets and an expansion in both capital and labour. The welfare state in Fordism is generally characterized as a bureaucratic and institutional response to the ills generated by the market economy (for example, occupational accidents and unemployment), providing social cohesion and a stable labour force to service capital (Jessop 1994; Pierson 1994). Most commentators agree that there is presently a transition from Fordist modes of production and accumulation, in which the 'rigidities' of Fordism are being replaced with post-Fordist 'flexibility' (Pierson 1994: 99). Within the economic and labour markets this flexibility is evidenced by deregulation and globalization. In welfare it is evidenced by a 'fundamental re-structuring of state interventionism' (Albertsen 1988: 349), as reviewed in Chapter 2 of this text, and the replacement of universalism with residualism. Welfare, including health care, is increasingly targeted at the self-actualizing, economically active and responsible citizen. Such citizens have both the economic and social capital to act upon health promotion, or to purchase insurance against ill-health through private health care schemes.

Purdy and Banks (1999) argue that this has resulted in a 'two nations' situation in which existing inequalities between rich and poor are exacerbated. Those with the poorest health have the most difficulty in accessing the healthy lifestyles promoted by government policy owing to low incomes, poor housing and inadequate diet. Such structural difficulties seriously impinge upon the choices of the individual (Purdy 1999). As Purdy (1999: 74) states, the emphasis upon 'governing the self' endemic to new welfare arrangements moves responsibility for health from the state to the individual. Health is no longer a 'right of citizenship, guaranteed by a welfare state', but is a 'duty of citizenship' aimed at alleviating the burden on the state and assisting the collective good. His prognosis for those who fail to regulate themselves is bleak. Ill-health will be characterized as 'moral failure', a self-inflicted risk by those too inadequate and unwilling to adopt healthy lifestyles.

New Labour proposals for health care in the Green Paper *Our Healthier Nation* (Department of Health 1998a) and in the subsequent Health Act 1999 reflect the Blairite adoption of 'Third Way' social policy as a response to the challenges of post-Fordism. Structural and environmental causes of ill-health are acknowledged, and a delicate balance between the avoidance of victim-blaming and 'nanny state social engineering' is sought (Department of Health 1998a: 28; Purdy 1999). Health risks are 'shared by society' and partnership is seen as the key to their effective management (Purdy 1999). However, individual responsibility for health risk management is still demanded. The healthy citizen is the 'socially responsible' citizen, and 'life-style management' is an essential ingredient of such responsibility.

'Advanced liberal' modes of governance and postmodernity

While the impact of postmodernity upon social policy and the organs of the welfare state remains debatable and unclear (Carter 1998), there is consensus that contemporary life is characterized by a preoccupation with risk (Beck 1992a; Giddens 1998a, b; Nettleton and Burrows 1998). A calculative atti-tude is a central feature of the individual's life in conditions of late modernity or postmodernity (Giddens 1991; Reddy 1996). There has to be a reflexive and self-monitoring attitude to life in which rational and informed choices about risk are essential. Such decisions almost inevitably involve decisions about 'lifestyle' and 'life-planning' and contribute to the structuring of our self-identity (Giddens 1991: 5). This notion of the active self is particularly significant in contemporary accounts of governance and social regulation (Rose 1993, 1996), and has implications in the health care arena (Petersen and Bunton 1997). Turner (1997: xviii) has argued that a risk society 'based upon deregulation and devolution . . . requires more subtle and systematic forms of control', not least self-control and self-regulation. He contends that two responses to the problematics of regulation can currently be discerned. The first is a flight from indeterminacy and uncertainty into a reassertion of Fordist policies and principles. Centrally formulated and implemented prescriptive policies are used to reduce uncertainty and unpre-dictability, and all agency activities are reduced to functional competencies and heavily monitored and controlled. This has been particularly acute in health care, social care and probation (Kemshall *et al.* 1997). This reflects a largely 'anticipationist' approach to risk, in which all possibilities are antici-pated and planned for (Hood *et al.* 1992). The result is prescription and standardization, and increased regulation by managers and policy-makers (Kemshall 1998). However, such an approach is both costly and ultimately self-defeating. All situations cannot be predicted, and constant monitoring and regulation of the activities of others, whether they be staff, managers, citizens or users, is time-consuming and requires ever more sophisticated systems and techniques (Hood and Jones 1996). Such an approach also stymies the 'resilient' risk culture desired by 'Third Way' advocates such as Giddens, who see risk taking and entrepreneurship as important responses to the late modern landscape (Giddens 1998a, b). Such anticipationism is what Turner (1997) disparagingly refers to as the 'McDonaldisation of risk'.

Theorists drawing upon the work of Michel Foucault (1965, 1970, 1973, 1977, 1991) have argued that late modern or postmodern society is characterized by an 'advanced liberalism' which embodies notions of self-governance and self-regulation (Rose 1993, 1996). Government is increasingly carried out through the activities of the socially responsible, self-regulating individual. Foucault's theory of power and his proffered relationship between the self and discipline have been significant in analysing these current trends (Burchell *et al.* 1991; Rose 1996; Petersen and Bunton 1997; Culpitt 1999). In brief, Foucault has explored the 'disciplinary power' utilized to govern the conduct of 'free individuals' (Dean 1994), and how 'free will' is directed and managed in society (Higgs 1998). This has been expressed in what Lupton (1995) and Higgs (1998) have characterized as an analysis: 'of the coercive and non-coercive strategies which the state and other institutions urge on individuals for their own benefit' (Higgs 1998: 185). Central to such strategies is the deployment of power through knowledge and the constitution of the individual as a site of self-management (Rose 2000). Expert knowledge, particularly within the social sciences, has played a significant role within the controlling mechanisms of welfare and health. Lupton notes that such a system of governmentality (that is, regulating conduct) is heavily dependent upon systems of expert knowledge which constitute and define the objects of their knowledge; for example, the 'policing of families' through childcare services (Donzelot 1980). The authority of the state is mediated by such welfare agencies, which set standards for acceptable conduct (the morally deserving family, the sentencing to 'treatment' of offenders). Such agencies can monitor compliance with societal norms through the delivery of social care and extend the surveillance net beyond the more obvious parameters of the police and the law (Foucault 1977). Such non-coercive and 'subtle' strategies enable Foucault to espouse an 'enabling' concept of power in which power produces actions and forms rather than merely limits them. 'Free will' is then understood as a phenomenon that is shaped and constituted by particular discourses and knowledge forms, and not as something that is merely dominated by the state.

Notions of appropriately deployed 'free will' and the exercise of the 'right choice' are central to the emerging mode of welfare provision. Miller and Rose (1990) have argued that the 'new citizen' of advanced liberal societies must exercise rational, informed personal choice on a range of issues:

> Programmes of government are to be evaluated in terms of the extent to which they enhance that choice. And the language of individual

freedom, personal choice and self-fulfilment has come to underpin programmes of government articulated across the political spectrum, from politicians and professionals, pressure groups and civil libertarians alike.

(Miller and Rose 1990: 24)

Such theorists argue that citizenship is now characterized by increased individualization and consumerism (Leonard 1997; Higgs 1998), along with increased social obligation and responsibilities (Giddens 1998b). It is the individual who is responsible for his or her actions, and for his or her future. Lifestyle and life-course are now viewed as within the individual's arena of choice, and as Petersen and Lupton (1996) put it, the individual is expected to make the 'right choice' and is punished or excluded for failing to do so. This displacement from state to individual avoids the problems of governance increasingly encountered by the late modern/postmodern 'flight from indeterminacy' (Turner 1997); that is, ever-increasing costly and ineffective regulation. However, present approaches to welfare can be characterized as a somewhat uncoordinated and unhappy mix of a retreat into Fordist certainties combined with attempts to engage with postmodern social forms – a blend of modern and postmodern (Kelly and Charlton 1995).

Surveillance and the regulation of lifestyles

Carter (1998: 23), in his critique of postmodern analyses of welfare provision, notes that 'Foucaultian notions of normalisation and surveillance are proposed as cultural constructs for the study of social policy', but he asks where the evidence is for their relevance to social policy. In health care the rise of health promotion is itself offered as evidence of a developing Foucauldian surveillance net. The displacement of health risk management from the state to the individual and from illness response to prevention is seen as a key feature of this development, along with an increased preoccupation with lifestyle regulation and management (Greco 1993; Lupton 1993, 1995; Bunton *et al.* 1995; Petersen 1994, 1996, 1997; Nettleton 1997; Petersen and Bunton 1997; Scrambler and Higgs 1998). Nettleton (1997: 210) has suggested that this has led to an 'explosion' of the 'epidemiological and medical literature' about those health risk factors 'over which the individual can have some control'. She cites the work of Skolbekken (1995), which noted the proliferation of 'risk articles' in British, American and Scandinavian medical journals between 1986 and 1991, during which time 80,000 were published in comparison to the 1000 per year in the preceding years. The British BIDS database shows that between 1997 and 2000 there were 98,512 articles on risk, and there were 1025 on risk and health promotion on the MEDLINE database.

What does this preoccupation with risk tell us about the surveillance and regulation of lifestyles? Bunton (1997) has argued that the interplay between risk management concerns and the promotion of self-care in recent health risk discourse is central to the emerging techniques of surveillance and regulation in postmodern society. He argues that two developments are key to the promotion of self-regulation: the internalization of risk into the consciousness of individuals (it is a *personal matter*); and the power of risk both to individualize and to aggregate (there are risky individuals as well as risky populations). Group risks have the power to marginalize and exclude, and Bunton cites drug users as a key example. Individual risks also have the power to define the self, either as excluded in the risky 'Other' or as included in the rational and prudential non-risky group. However, risks are diverse and choices endless. The prudential individual is confronted daily with multiple risk decisions, requiring what Giddens (1991) has called reflexivity, or the notion of constantly reviewing one's options, one's lifestyle and one's life-plan. As Bunton (1997: 230) puts it, 'Self-actualisation is understood in terms of a balance between opportunity and risk.'

In health care this is epitomized by the emphasis upon citizens who are 'active and enterprising' in the maintenance of their own bodies and their own health (Bunton 1997: 241). The reward is not only lower private health insurance against risk, but also moral worth and virtue as an enterprising citizen. However, such citizens cannot be understood as merely 'cultural dopes' (Giddens 1984) taking uncritical direction from health promotion. According to Nettleton, the relationship between citizens and experts is far more complex. She argues that:

> most people do not simply passively accept the pronouncements of medical 'experts' who may be equipped with varying forms of technological equipment; these are simply resources which individuals or 'consumers' are able to draw upon, or reject, when reflecting upon their lifestyles. Government requires the 'risky selves' to be wise about their investments . . . Governments, policy-makers, and other institutions and agencies can provide the 'facts' but ultimately it is individuals who decide, select and act upon them.
>
> (Nettleton 1997: 216)

'Facts' are mediated by individuals, and expert knowledge can be disputed, challenged or rejected. However, the 'right choice' is central to the appropriate construction of the self as normal, and the distinction of self from excluded and stigmatized others. Brown has demonstrated this in respect of acquired immunodeficiency syndrome (AIDS) and the role of public health campaigns in acting to '(re)produce stigmatising boundaries between so-called "at risk" and "normal" populations' (T. Brown 2000: 1274). Brown argues that the pursuit of normal health has legitimized the extension of health promotion and its regulatory practices to the population at large, a key tactic in social governance. Such governance is dependent upon what Rose (2000) has described as 'responsibilisation'; that is, individuals are made responsible for their own actions, including their own risks, and for their own effective self-management. A consequence of such responsibilization is individual blame when risks do occur or are ill-managed. Such victim-blaming has manifested itself within health care, particularly in the delineation of self-inflicted risks. Early responses to AIDS exemplified such victim-blaming (Crawford 1994; Kingham 1997). AIDS in particular was transformed from a viral infection to a 'plague', constituted in the media as a 'gay plague' terrifying (presumably 'normal') citizens, and a siege mentality was typically presented in the early stages of AIDS media reporting (Karpf 1988). The proliferation of potentially 'at-risk' groups in the later stages of the AIDS epidemic drew more groups into the realm of the stigmatized 'Other' (Waldby 1996), and legitimated the extension of health promotion, with its emphasis upon 'good health', to the whole population (Petersen and Lupton 1996). AIDS is a specific example of the contribution of health promotion to techniques of self-governance. However, health promotion can be understood within the broader context of advanced liberal governmentality, in which risk and responsibilization are meshed as key mechanisms of self-regulation (Petersen 1996; Nettleton 1997; T. Brown 2000).

Summary

Health promotion has become a key site for risk concerns in current health care policy and represents a key shift from a needs-led medical model of universal health provision to a risk-led model which emphasizes self-care, lifestyle choice and self-risk management. The development can be seen in terms both of a response to post-Fordist challenges to universal welfare, and of the self-regulation required by advanced liberal modes of government. Central to such a mode of government is the exercise of 'free will' within 'expertly' constructed modes of knowledge and discourse, of which health promotion is a powerful example. Costly overt state regulation is displaced to individual self-regulation, with 'choice', particularly as exercised by the prudential, socially obligated citizen, central to such regulation. While expertise may be mediated and challenged, the 'right choices' are none the less promoted, and the self-actualizing citizen acting with social obligation towards the collective good is expected to make them. Failure to do so risks blame and exclusion.

The rise of private medical insurance, risk and rationing

The NHS has been subject to change throughout its short history (Levitt and Wall 1992). Recent years have, however, seen unprecedented change, reminiscent of Giddens's 'runaway world' in which the pace of social change imposes constant reorganization upon institutional forms and social structures (Giddens 1991: 16). In health care this has seen the dismantling of the bureaucratic national health care system in favour of internal markets and a 'mixed economy' of provision involving both the private and voluntary sectors alongside the statutory (Walby and Greenwell 1994). The restructuring of the 1980s (the 'Thatcher years') saw the introduction of cash limits, performance indicators, efficiency standards, competitive tendering and contracting out, and the replacement of 'patients' with 'consumers' through the introduction of *The Patient's Charter* (Department of Health 1991a). While some commentators, such as Klein (1995), have argued that despite such wholesale restructuring the key principle of universal provision remained untouched, but the restructuring opened the way for the marketization and privatization of health care provision. By the 1990s how to provide and pay for universal health care was a burgeoning issue, promoting consideration of various mechanisms of provision and payment. These included:

- maintenance of a free service at point of delivery (Allsop 1997);
- additional charging (accommodation, for example) (Goldsmith 1997);
- compulsory savings in 'Medisave accounts' (Ham 1997);
- the development of non-profitable charitable trusts (Green 1997);
- the creation of a semi-independent public corporation;
- the use of 'hypothecated taxes' – that is, taxes which go directly to the NHS (Milburn 2000a).

Alongside concerns with how to fund public sector health care, there has been a rise in private health care provision. As Green (1985) has pointed out, private health care is nothing new. Pre-Beveridge, numerous systems for paying for health care existed, including mutual and friendly societies, trade union assistance and private insurance. Lloyd George's 1911 National Insurance Act had its roots in the friendly society system and provided a national system of cover against a range of risks for working people. This scheme was gradually extended, and the post-war implementation of the National Health Service represented the extension of collective insurance against individual risks to all. The history of the NHS saw health care costs grow as a proportion of gross national product (GDP) from just over 3 per cent in 1960 to 6.6 per cent by the close of the century. Private sector provision also grew sharply in this period (Clark *et al.* 1995). While Britain's health care costs as a proportion of GDP are well below the average for Western economies (Clark *et al.* 1995), the NHS is subject to almost annual 'funding crises'. The accumulated debt of the NHS is now estimated at £1 billion (Barkham 2000).

The rise of private medical insurance

The private sector, particularly as funded by insurance schemes, has been proposed as one mechanism for bridging the gap between public demand for health care and the state's ability to provide it. As Clark *et al.* (1995) point out, the NHS is now challenged by an ageing population and demands for long-term care, and the growing expectations of the public fed in large part by technological advances in medicine. This has been paralleled by a 'results culture', in which outcomes in terms of both targets on waiting lists and clinical effectiveness are given greater weight. Consumer choice and rights have also contributed to public expectations, in terms not only of access to treatment, but also of its timeliness and excellence. Private medical provision through insurance had reached 10 per cent of NHS hospital budgets by 1995, with company purchase of insurance for employees forming a significant part of all medical insurance bought (Clark *et al.* 1995). Private work in NHS hospitals rose from £77.6 million in 1988/9 to £198.2 million by 1994/5 (Brindle 1996). By 1996 the NHS was the largest provider of pay beds (Cervi 1996).

While the distribution of private medical insurance (PMI) is uneven, driven by affluence, demographic factors and geographical location, one key factor in the growth of medical insurance is perceived dissatisfaction with the NHS (Clark *et al.* 1995). It is perhaps significant that the fastest growth in PMI was during the restructuring of the 1980s, when the NHS was subject to fiscal restraint, large waiting lists, treatment delays and low morale. Availability is also a key factor, with a growing perception that the NHS is retrenching to core treatment and emergency medicine, with alternative treatments, 'peripheral' treatments like *in vitro* fertilization and long-term palliative care moving to the private sector. By the 1990s the private and public sector were inextricably linked (Clark *et al.* 1995), with NHS hospitals receiving private sector funding through pay beds and many fund-holding general practitioners utilizing the private insurance of patients to preserve funds. They see the future financing and development of health care as dependent upon two issues: efficiency and equity. Concerns for efficient operation and equitable distribution and access have been seen as legitimate constraints upon the operation of an unregulated market for health care (Barr 1992). Key limits upon the efficient operation of PMI are:

- the short-sightedness of individuals, which results in under-insurance (for example, the failure to insure adequately for old age);
- the high costs of palliative care;
- the exclusion of some high-risk groups owing to the anticipated high costs of treatment (for example, AIDS);
- the *moral hazard* of over-consumption of unnecessary health care driven by both patients and health care professionals.

The resulting inefficiencies become costs, and these are translated into higher premium costs. Clark *et al.* note that the steadying in the rate of PMI take-up in the late 1980s and early 1990s was owing in part to the higher premium costs incurred and the lower take-up of company policies as costs became prohibitive. In terms of equity, PMI is also dependent upon ability and willingness to pay, and one's health risk rating. Some groups, such as the low paid, unemployed and chronically sick, are effectively excluded. 'Bad risks' are not insured.

Despite the persistence of health inequalities (Black *et al.* 1980; Purdy and Banks 1999), principles of universal access and equity are seen as central to the provision of health care. The 1994 British Social Attitudes Survey (Jowell 1994) found that 55 per cent of the general public thought that health care provision should be the same for all. While the NHS has espoused this, in principle it has been difficult to achieve. Free health care at point of delivery based upon medical need has been the key underpinning principle of the NHS (Culyer and Wagstaff 1992). However, treatment by post code, class, social and occupational inequalities and geographical disparities in health care and the health care status of individuals have belied this (Purdy and Banks 1999). Similarly, PMI cannot guarantee equity owing to the 'adverse selection' of bad risks and the exclusion of some of the most sick and needy. In recent years there has been a shift in equity considerations from a medical needs-led model to an emphasis upon health status and attention to the causal factors of ill-health rather than treatment. This was introduced primarily through the government document *The Health of the Nation* (Department of Health 1992) and subsequently reinforced under New Labour with *Our Healthier Nation* (Department of Health 1998a), and has spawned a growing emphasis upon health promotion (as discussed above). There are significant implications for PMI as well as the public sector in this move. The emphasis upon prevention and self-risk management is likely to increase the growing consumerist approach to health, in which PMI will continue to have a role in meeting personal choice and insuring against future ills (Nettleton 1997). Preventative medicine in the PMI arena is likely to manifest itself in terms of health risk screening as individuals seek to self-regulate their own health (for example, 'well woman' clinics), and also in occupational and company screening of current and prospective employees in an effort to screen out 'bad risks'. As National Health Service priorities have become more transparent, and differences between peripheral, elective and core treatments are drawn (Health Committee First Report 1994–5), PMI could be deployed as a 'top-up' for those treatments not normally available through the NHS (Clark *et al.* 1995). Fertility treatment is one such example. Such an approach is of course dependent upon clear distinctions between core and peripheral treatments, distinguishing between those which are essential and those which are merely desirable. Despite the recommendations of the Commission for Social Justice (1994), these distinctions have yet to be finely drawn. In effect, this would represent a statement on the health risks that the public sector would bear, and those that would become the preserve of private provision. This may represent an opportunity for the state to redistribute risks – for example, the costs of illness and palliative care associated with old age – to the insurance market as public sector residential and hospital provision for this 'market' shrinks.

While the private and public sectors are likely to continue to coexist, the question remains about the distribution of health risks across the two sectors, and more importantly how the public sector can meet rising demand with limited resources. This necessarily leads to considerations of rationing, and how best both to restructure and to ration health care provision for the twenty-first century.

Rationing and risks

Continual funding difficulties and the restructuring of the NHS have made both the prioritizing and rationing of health care more transparent. The introduction of the internal market, coupled with a mixed economy of provision, introduced economic values into health care, with an increased emphasis upon audit, fiscal control, planning, and input-output measures (National Audit Office 1994). Wall and Owen (1999: 48) note that since the extension of its remit to cover health, the Audit Commission has carried out over 40 investigations, including 'GP prescribing practices, improving Accident and Emergency services, and measuring management costs'. Financing the NHS, in terms of the amount of money that should be provided and whether such money is being put to best use, has become a major issue and prey to political as well as economic considerations. Cost–benefit calculations and the Resource Management Initiative, coupled with the introduction of the internal market, focused attention on the *efficient* use of resources throughout the 1980s and early 1990s (Wall and Owen 1999). More recently, concerns have turned to reducing waiting lists (Toynbee 2000), and to considerations of *effectiveness* through clinical audit (National Audit Office 1994). All these measures have been aimed at controlling ever-increasing health care costs. As Wall and Owen put it,

> If those in charge were unable to force through efficiency, and if those actually spending the resources were not particularly interested in efficiency (at least in terms understood by the politicians), then the impersonal laws of the market place would do the job instead.
>
> (Wall and Owen 1999: 45)

However, market controls have failed to reduce spending. Alongside considerations of funding (how much and in what form), considerations of what *type* of service and how it should be allocated have arisen – in other words, rationing. In reality health care has been prioritized for some time, with some patients receiving treatment sooner than others. Priority setting is of course a form of rationing, and to date the waiting list has been the major mechanism of rationing. In this system cases are dealt with according to their urgency based upon a medical needs-led model imposed by health care professionals (usually consultants). The model has come increasingly under challenge as waiting lists have become a subject of public discontent and political attention (Barkham 2000). Professional bias and self-interest and class, gender and geographical inequalities have all been implicated in the construction of waiting lists (Allsop 1995; Purdy and Banks 1999). This has resulted in a concern for a more rational and transparent rationing mechanism for the NHS (Bourlet 1994; Health Committee First Report 1994–5) to avoid the apparent lottery by doctors and 'post code' (Macdonald 1996).

Two formal mechanisms for rationing health care have been proposed: the 'Oregon model' and the 'quality adjusted life year' (QALY) formula. The Oregon model derives from a restructuring of Medicaid provision in Oregon, USA (Baggott 1998). The system represents a retrenchment of provision back to cost-effective, clinically beneficial treatments in order to extend the provision to more people. To do this, treatments with low survival rates were withdrawn, and treatments were subject to cost–benefit analysis. In addition, members of the public were consulted about the nature of core provision and what should be excluded. While difficulties with the model exist, not least how to decide between differing public (or consumer) views, the model does introduce important key principles: the use of a 'rational' and transparent distinction between core and peripheral treatments; and cost–benefit analysis of clinical effectiveness as the basis for treatment interventions.

The QALY formula calculates both likely survival time and quality of life improvement in the assessment of treatment interventions and can compare the same treatment for different patients, and different treatments for different conditions (Baggott 1998). Clinical audits of effectiveness and economic calculations of treatment costs are integral to this approach. However, such an approach can discriminate against vulnerable groups, such as the mentally ill or the elderly, resulting in public disquiet and media criticism when treatment is withheld (for example, the use of 'do not resuscitate orders' on the elderly).

Both models challenge a universal needs-led approach to health care, and, through differing mechanisms, reduce public sector health care to a residual system in which only 'good risks' are backed. However, even previous exponents of the market such as Peter Lilley, Social Services Secretary under Margaret Thatcher, have cautioned against such an approach, recognizing that the chronically sick, for example, are 'virtually uninsurable' and would be excluded from treatment under both the above models (*Guardian* 1999). In effect, the question is whether health risks should be pooled and dealt with through the collective system of taxation, or whether they should be individualized and dealt with through a combination of economic and insurance systems based on health status.

Summary

The costs of both public and private sector health care have grown during the lifetime of the NHS. PMI in particular has been seen as one possibility for bridging the gap between public demand and state shortfalls in provision. However, PMI is limited by premium costs, ability and willingness to pay, under-insurance by consumers, moral hazard and adverse selection. While public support for the NHS remains strong, PMI has a strong foothold in 'queue jumping' for elective treatments and for the purchase of non-NHS treatments such as *in vitro* fertilization. The major contribution of PMI to the NHS debate has not been in terms of a realistic alternative to all public sector provision, but in the development of actuarially calculated risks to health provision, particularly the notion of bad risks and adverse selection, and in the economic costing of treatments. This has helped to extend the funding debate from *how* to *what*, and raises the possibility of transforming the NHS from a universal to a residual service, with the possibility of redistributing some risks away from the public sector. In effect, the debate is now on what should be provided and in what form, as well as how it should be funded.

Health care in the new millennium: the modernization process

Throughout the history of the NHS there have been two main responses to the challenge of delivering health care. The first approach, pursued exten- sively in the 1980s, was 'sector reform'; that is, a deliberate shift away from public provision to a mixed economy including the voluntary and private sectors (Wall and Owen 1999). This period saw the introduction of the internal market, privatization and a 'new managerialism' to cut away the last vestiges of monolithic bureaucracy (Clarke and Newman 1997). The second approach is characterized by a shift away from hospital provision to primary care and prevention, and is epitomized by the new public health movement of the 1990s. It is against this backdrop that New Labour entered office in 1997 with a mission to modernize and reform the NHS. The White Paper *The New NHS* in 1997 offered a 'third way . . . a new model for the new century. There will be neither a return to the old centralized command and control systems of the 1970s, nor a continuation of the divisive internal market system of the 1990s' (Department of Health 1997: para. 2.1). The White Paper emphasized:

- the transformation of the internal market into a system of commissioning and providing, and the replacement of the purchaser–provider relationship with three-year service agreements;
- the establishment of Primary Care Groups to replace GP fund-holding;
- reduction in the number of health authorities and a requirement for local Health Improvement Programmes;
- emphasis upon collaboration, quality assurance and evidence-based practice;
- emphasis upon partnership in service delivery (Wall and Owen 1999).

The subsequent 1999 Health Act enacted these core proposals through:

- the creation of primary care trusts;
- emphasis upon quality and evidence-based practice;
- partnership and cooperation;
- the establishment of the Commission for Health Improvement;
- increased governance and regulation of the medical profession and health care professionals.

The Act represents a considerable restructuring of the NHS, and shifts the rationale of provision from a largely hospital-based service to a more holistic approach to health care in which health promotion and cooperative partnerships between various providers at local and national level are stressed. Quality of care and the appropriate mechanisms to increase the health of the nation are emphasized at the expense of traditional curative principles. Clinical governance (that is, the regulation of clinical conduct and standards) and professional regulation are introduced by the Act, and have continued to be seen as key components of NHS modernization (Blair 2000a, b). Increasingly modernization has been the price of increased funding. In a series of key interviews on the future of the NHS, Tony Blair stated that the choice for British health care was between 'a shift to an American-style system in which people would be guaranteed treatment only for emergencies' or reform of the NHS (Miles and Baldwin 2000). The Prime Minister's announcement of a ten-year plan for the NHS, including increased spending, was accompanied by proposals for a modernization programme to be unveiled in July 2000 (Taylor 2000). Such proposals are aimed at ending traditional working systems, changing professional demarcation boundaries (for example, between doctors and nurses) and planning to make the NHS more cost-efficient. The modernization programme represents a 'Third Way' attempt to transform the remaining monolith of the NHS into a flexible and adaptable organization fit for the twenty-first century. This modernization process has been described by some commentators as nothing less than a 'second Beveridge' (C. Brown 2000). The emphasis in health care is clearly shifting, with the 'new NHS' focusing on primary care, health promotion, health improvement and modernization of both the infrastructure of health care delivery and the practices of health care professionals.

The implications for health professionals

Modernization, risk and rationing are presenting real challenges to health care professionals at the beginning of the twenty-first century. Modernization presents challenges to traditional work practices, boundaries and demarcations in health care delivery, with increased emphasis upon 'flexibility', 'multiskilling', 'team work' and the removal of professional restrictions upon service delivery. Central to such modernization is increased regulation and governance of health care staff, in particular doctors and consultants. This has resulted in greater attention to standards, quality assurance and enforcement of codes of conduct. Audit has played a considerable part in both establishing and enforcing quality standards, and while the activities of the Audit Commission have been wide ranging (Wall and Owen 1999), it has also encompassed clinical audit. Such audits are concerned with the critical evaluation of the outcomes of clinical diagnosis and subsequent interventions. Traditionally subject to peer review, clinical audit is now seen as the appropriate preserve of formalized quality assurance and risk management systems. In a climate of litigation, public blame and media accountability, clinical care and its governance are subject to heightened scrutiny (Powell 2000). Quality clinical care is seen as protection against potential risks and liability (National Health Service Management Executive (NHSME) 1993). Risks arising from working practices, as opposed to those arising from physical or environmental hazards, have attracted attention, not least owing to increased litigation and public outcry (NHSME 1993). The internal self-regulation of the professionals involved is no longer seen as an appropriate risk management mechanism (Health Act 1999; see Davies 2000).

In addition to increased concerns with internally produced risks, health care has also been confronted with broader risks to the 'health of the nation' and with the risky choices and behaviours of citizens. The requirement to improve the health of the nation has increased the attention to public health, health promotion, primary care and partnerships. The pattern of health care provision is changing in response to these demands and it is clear that New Labour expects workers to adapt (Blair 2000a). Modernization has been accompanied by increased funding, with the NHS set for an unprecedented period of growth, double that which it has enjoyed over the past 25 years. Blair's Third Way solution to the NHS has been seen as a reiteration of the state's commitment to universal health care provision (Mitchell 1997), and an avoidance of the difficult issue of rationing (Wall and Owen 1999). However, rationing is unlikely to be as easily resolved. The history of the NHS is one of ever-increasing demand and finite resources. The displacement of front-line health care to a combination of primary care and health promotion may merely mask rationing issues, and displace the responsibility for rationing decisions from national politicians to local managers and the individual citizen. New Labour's approach to the NHS is characterized more by modernization – that is, pragmatic adaptation of existing structures – than by root and branch radicalism (Paton 1999). Such pragmatic adaptability poses reform and increased accountability for expenditure as key themes, but at the bottom avoids the more politically challenging question of rationing. New Labour emphasizes that the NHS is a value for money service 'because it invests in the health of the workforce to the economic benefit of all, but also because it does so cheaply . . . and the new healthcare state is about direct investment in productivity' (Paton 1999: 73).

Conclusions

Harris and McDonald (2000) have argued that the case for postmodern welfare should be subject to an empirical test prior to making wholesale claims for transition. So what is the case for transition in health care? While the case for a wholesale shift to a residual service cannot be fully made, there is substantial evidence for a growing emphasis upon risk and Third Way solutions in the provision of health. The 1990s shift to new public health and the current modernization programme represent key trends in reframing conceptions of health care provision, what should constitute such provision and how it should be delivered. These trends have been gaining momentum and are set to continue under New Labour's modernization programme. Partnership and 'responsibilization' have become central principles in the provision of health care, enabling a lessening of a centralized bureaucratic system of delivery. Changes are certainly taking place, particularly in the displacement of health care responsibility to local management structures and individuals, a phenomenon Cochrane (1994) has labelled 'locality planning'. Whether these changes are indicative of a post-Fordist health care system is less clear (Cochrane 1994), although the current modernization process has features of a post-Fordist welfare state (Burrows and Loader 1994). Allandale (1998: 197), for example, sees NHS modernization as a product of post-Fordist economic regulation in which services must 'innovate to meet the demands of an ever-changing consumer market'. For some commentators New Labour's approach to the NHS is the area in which the Third Way is less in evidence, with policy lurching awkwardly between reform and retention of conservative policies and structures (Paton 1999).

Distinguishing between Third Way rhetoric and reality requires evidence of change. However, Harris and McDonald (2000) have reminded us that such processes of change are mediated by existing organizational forms and institutional arrangements. The NHS is no exception. Professional autonomy and vested interest have limited both the pace and extent of change since the inception of the NHS in 1948 (Wall and Owen 1999). This 'second Beveridge' is already facing resistance (*Guardian* 2000a), leading the Secretary of State to comment that money alone was not enough to transform the NHS, but that 'policing' standards, clinical governance and the reduction of consultant power would all be necessary (Milburn 2000b). The further modernization of the NHS is likely to consist of a twin-track approach to reform, consisting of a restructuring of modes of delivery and reform of the work practices of health care professionals. At the time of writing further NHS reforms were announced by the Prime Minister (Blair 2000b). These included:

- extra provision in terms of beds and personnel;
- the creation of an NHS modernization agency;
- closer partnership between health and social services;
- changes in terms and conditions of employment for some NHS staff, such as consultants;
- increase in patients' choice and rights;
- electronic records;
- reduced waiting times and the future introduction of a booking system;
- reduction of health inequalities, reduction in treatment by post code and increased cancer screening and treatment;
- higher standards of care for the elderly;
- increase in number of private rooms (from *Guardian* 2000b).

'At a glance' the reforms reflect New Labour's modernization agenda, with emphasis upon 'joined up' provision epitomized by partnership, reform of role boundaries and conditions of employment, increases in standards and quality of service provision, and increased accountability. According to Paton (2000), this constitutes a 'sharpening up' of the NHS in the new post-Fordist climate. While some countries have eschewed direct provision of health services, Paton argues that New Labour has recognized that Britain has a 'ready-made instrument for investing in the health of the productive, cheaply – the NHS' (p. 30). Britain is prepared to continue to invest in the productive through direct public sector provision such as the NHS, but such investment does not necessarily mean equity (Exworthy and Powell 2000; Paton 2000).

The NHS remains at heart one of the last vestiges of universal welfare provision, albeit much subject to modernization and reform. Risk and responsibilization are growing themes particularly evidenced by the emphasis upon health promotion, disease prevention, self-care and self-regulation. Risks and rationing are also subject to closer linkage, in terms of private health care provision, but also through the overt introduction of economic considerations into health care and the emphasis upon value for money and effective treatment. Clinical audit and governance are as much about rationing towards effective treatment as they are about promoting good practice (for example, the National Institute of Clinical Excellence), and evidence-based practice has become a cornerstone of both clinical governance and clinical audit (Harrison and Wood 2000). While the NHS has not yet been transformed from a universal to a residual service, the debate is no longer about how to continue to fund the NHS on an incremental basis. Instead it is about what should be provided (and what should not), and how it should be delivered.

Note

1 See Chapter 9 of Wall and Owen (1999) for a full review.

Suggestions for further reading

Hann, A. (2000) *Analysing Health Policy*. Aldershot: Ashgate. This edited work provides a useful overview of New Labour developments in health policy, including a chapter on 'Third Way' approaches to health care.

Petersen, A. and Bunton, R. (1997) *Health and Medicine*. London: Routledge. This edited work provides a key introduction to Foucauldian and postmodern theories of health. Risk is particularly well covered in Chapters 10 and 11.

chapter

four

Child protection and the care of the elderly: need, vulnerability and risk

Introduction

New Labour social policy has tended to emphasize the 'good' spend of positive welfare such as education, training and workfare, and the personal social services have received rather less attention (Johnson 1999). However, two areas have attracted public and media attention and reform: child protection and 'care of the elderly'. Child deaths under social services supervision (Jasmine Beckford: London Borough of Brent 1985), child abuse within local authority children's homes and public disquiet over child protection procedures (e.g. Cleveland: Butler Schloss 1988) have raised public awareness of social services provision to children and families. As Johnson points out, this is somewhat at odds with the actual numbers of children concerned and related resources. In 1995, 57,000 children were being looked after by local authorities in England, Wales and Northern Ireland, with 38,000 of them on child protection registers (Johnson 1999: 79).

The growing elderly population and the burgeoning costs of care for this group have focused both public and political attention on 'care of the elderly'. By the early 1990s there were approximately 8.8 million people over 65, with around 10 million pensioners (Meredith 1993). Of greater concern is the projected 1 million persons expected to live beyond 85 years beyond the year 2000 (Livesley and Crown 1992). In 2001 life expectancy for women will be 80 and 75 for men, and by 2040 there will be only two people working for every pensioner (Age Concern 2000). Spiralling costs of residential and nursing home care have also caused concern, both for those subjected to means testing and for government. As Browne (1996: 52) points out, 'Between 1979 and 1991 the amount of money claimed to support individuals in residential and nursing homes grew from £10 million to £1,872 million and the number of claimants grew from 12,000 to 231,000 (Wistow *et al.* 1994).' When the welfare state was initiated, 60 per cent of the population was under 20; by 2020 this will have reduced to less than 25 per cent. Actuarial predictions of life expectancy at the inception of the National Health Service were for only three years of life after retirement; currently ten years plus is far from unusual (Age Concern 2000). By 1997 there were 307,000 older persons in residential homes, and based upon a survey week in September 1997, Johnson (1999: 79) highlights the further provision of 746,000 'meals on wheels' and 2.6 million hours of home-care for 470,000 households, 632,000 day centre places and 490,000 attendances. While these seem to represent massive provision, Johnson reminds us that most people will not need to use the personal social services even within these target client groups. In this sense, child protection and care of the elderly are already residual services. Older persons in particular are often the subjects of 'DIY welfare' (Klein and Millar 1995) through privately purchased services or through the informal care of family carers. The cost of long-term care has also taxed government. In its response to the Royal Commission on Long-Term Care for the Elderly chaired by Sir Steward Sutherland, the government clearly stated that 'Older people are not, and must never be seen as, a burden on society', but that 'our ageing society creates a new set of challenges to which we must rise' (Department of Health 2000: 3). The Commission has proposed that personal care (as opposed to health care or social care) should be free at point of delivery, with living and housing costs remaining means-tested (Royal Commission 1999), although dissenting voices on the Commission argued that the costs of personal care would be unaffordable in the long term (McCurry 1999). The Commission was torn between wishing to provide universal benefit and more accurately targeting the poorest pensioners (Steele 1999). The proposed NHS plan steers a mid-course between rejecting state provision and assuming the full 'burden'. A compromise position emphasizing prevention of ill-health, flexible services to avoid unnecessary hospital admissions and 'intermediate care' at home is advocated. Partnership and 'integrated services' are seen as the key to enhanced value for money, and emphasis is placed upon finding a 'fairer and lasting balance between taxpayers and individuals . . . for the funding of long term care' (Department of Health 2000: 5).

The changing face of the personal social services

Kemshall *et al.* (1997) have argued that the personal social services are increasingly characterized by their preoccupation with the assessment and management of risk. Within a broader frame of the 'risk society', they argue that these risk preoccupations can be assigned to specific developments, such as:

- the requirement to ration and more effectively to use resources;
- increased accountability for service delivery and worker activities;
- the requirement to balance freedom and choice with harm reduction and risk management (Kemshall *et al.* 1997: 219).

These developments have their roots within the New Right critique of welfarism and, in terms of the personal social services, the Thatcherite attack on a social work profession characterized as 'self-serving' (Cochrane 1993). The New Right critique comprised four key features: cost, distaste for the 'nanny state' and the dependency culture created, deinstitutionalization of residential care to the community and the deprofessionalization of social work to lower-paid local authority workers or to the voluntary sector (Cochrane 1993). Finally, the role of the local authority social services department was transformed from primary provider of welfare to the purchasing and coordinating of care services. The introduction of community care through the NHS and Community Care Act 1990 transformed social workers from professional providers of social work services to practical case managers (Department of Health 1990a). Local authority provision became 'care in the community', and not only *in* the community but also *by* the community in the form of voluntary agencies and private services.

Care in the community

While initially conceptualized as a programme of deinstitutionalization from residential care, particularly for children, those with learning disabilities and the mentally ill, care in the community has also become synonymous with residual state care, partnership, contracting in and self-care. From the 1960s onwards deinstitutionalization was posed as a worthy social care aim, particularly of large and inhumane psychiatric hospitals, but was given added impetus in the 1980s by the Griffiths Report (1988). This noted that community care lacked reality and was 'everybody's poor relation but nobody's baby' (para. 9). The report's recommendations integrated concerns with meeting needs as defined by clients with meeting them in the local community with 'the least disruption to ordinary living' and in the most cost-effective way (pp. 5–6). Cost, need and deinstitutionalization were thereby fused. The report proposed a comprehensive system of community care in which social services social work departments would adopt a strategic and co-ordinating role, 'identifying needs and purchasing services from a range of other agencies, groups and even individuals' (Cochrane 1993: 78). The Conservative government finally took up the proposals, not least because they followed an earlier Audit Commission (1986) report that questioned the extent of state provision in social care. The Griffiths Report subsequently became the White Paper *Caring for People: Community Care in the Next Decade and Beyond* (Department of Health 1989), and finally the NHS and Community Care Act 1990. The latter was subjected to a staged implementation from April 1991 to April 1993 in order to prevent the escalation of community charge levels (Wistow *et al.* 1994).

The Act introduced a purchaser–provider split and transformed social workers into the commissioners and coordinators of a range of services from varied sources. The earlier Barclay Report (1982) had highlighted that the bulk of social care in England and Wales was provided by 'ordinary people' through 'informal caring networks', and that a partnership between such networks and statutory services could provide more care in the community. The 1980s saw the post-Second World War desegregation and deinstitutionalization of social care increase (Pilgrim and Johnson 1993), paralleled by the New Right challenge to the 'old consensus' on universal welfare provision (Powell and Hewitt 1998). The 'Thatcher years' saw a strategic change in the role of social services from main providers to a co-ordinating role for services provided from elsewhere, and to core provision of those 'services that no-one else could or would take on' (Walker 1993: 204). The NHS and Community Care Act epitomized this residualism, with its emphasis upon tight resourcing and value for money, and, despite the rhetoric of choice, carers were still to be the passive receivers of managerially determined 'care packages' (Walker 1993). Langan (1990: 58–9) has described it as an era of 'austerity and privatisation', synthesizing the 'principles of a free market with the attitudes of a strong state'. Welfare provision was reconstituted as a market product through competitive tendering and a mixed economy of provision (Department of Health 1989). While Griffiths had recommended a 'level playing field' between the statutory and private sectors, market conditions inevitably resulted in a creaming off of 'the less severely disabled and less costly users, leaving a rump of the most severely disabled in the public sector' (Walker 1993: 212). Assessments were driven by rationing, resources and eligibility, rather than by user choice (Langan 1990). While flexibility in meeting individual need was emphasized by Griffiths, this has since come to have a rhetorical and residual meaning. As Doyal (1993) has argued, the current structure of community care operates at a minimal level of need rather than an optimal one: the least required for 'physical health and autonomy' rather than the optimal levels required for quality of life and positive citizenship.

Establishing and meeting legitimate need has continued to dog community care provision throughout the late 1980s and 1990s. This has been particularly acute in the care of the elderly, with the burgeoning costs of long-term care drawing sharp attention to the role of state provision. The means testing of local authority social security department residential care has received much criticism (Walker 1993), not least from older service users. The announcement by the then Conservative Health Secretary Stephen Dorrell in May 1996 that people should use private insurance to pay for care in their old age was greeted by the press as the 'end of the welfare state' (Brindle 1996). As Glennerster (1999) has put it, the protection of those universal services that command public support and the votes of the middle class are going to cost money. The 'Third Way' solution is to reduce the spend on 'bad' services such as social security, promote private alternatives (for example, private pensions) and retreat to a core of preferred services such as health and education. However, as Johnson has pointed out, New Labour's treatment of the personal social services and community care has been ambivalent. Some areas of continuity with the preceding Conservative administration can be discerned. Internal markets and a mixed economy of social care are accepted, and while 'best value' and 'benchmarking' may have replaced competitive tendering, value for money in service provision is still evident. Spending has also increased, providing an extra £2.2 billion to local authorities (Comprehensive Spending Review 1998), though this has been largely targeted at provision most likely to gain public support (for example, increased community supervision of the mentally ill and long-term care of the elderly). The White Paper *Modernising Social Services* (Department of Health 1998b) committed additional funds (some £3 billion) but also outlined the 'Third Way to social care' in which modernization was seen as essential (Chapter 1), and a 'best value performance management framework' (Chapter 7) for increasing performance and accountability. The extent of this continuity in social policy across the political parties has led some social policy commentators to pose a 'new welfare consensus' (Deacon 1996; Powell and Hewitt 1998). New welfare is characterized by pragmatism in policy-making, a consumerist approach to provision and an acceptance of residualism in the interests of economic growth. A welfare system based upon a universal guarantee of a 'national minimum' is slowly being replaced by a system based upon selection and conditionality. Tony Blair set out the selection criteria when he launched his campaign for welfare reform: 'that anyone in genuine need would be helped; anyone capable of working should work; and that individuals should provide for themselves when able to do so' (in Green 1998). Rights of the state were to be more closely linked to the duties of citizenship (Blair 1998b). Welfare services would be delivered through a 'partnership of public and private sectors' (Blair 1998b). Jordan (2000: 25) has characterized this as the 'tough love' of social work, in which 'service providers must expect more from service users, must test their eligibility for services more strictly' and generally encourage independence. In the regime of tough love, 'reciprocity', 'responsible community' and mutuality are emphasized (Jordan 2000: 37).

Services are also conditional upon both genuine need and the rights and duties of citizenship within an active welfare state that emphasizes a 'hand up', not a 'hand out' (Powell and Hewitt 1998). The state's contract with the individual is that something will only be provided for something, and perverse incentives to remain dependent are discouraged (Giddens 1998b). The application of such an approach is easily discernible in the realms of workfare and benefit fraud, but what are its implications for community care provision to those groups excluded from the labour market and for whom 'dependency' is a fact of life?

The creation of dependency: childhood and old age

Corby (1993: 7) in an important work on child abuse, reminds us of the 'socially constructed nature of childhood'. Childhood as a phenomenon located within specific historical and social discourse is now increasingly accepted (Moss *et al.* 2000). While the common-sense view of childhood is of an age-related phenomena, often reflected in legal rights and laws such as the age of criminal responsibility, or the age of consent to sexual intercourse, views of childhood and the subsequent treatment of children can vary across countries and cultures. Some children under 16 will be subject to compulsory education, while in other areas of the globe similarly aged children will have been active in the workforce for some time. The former tend to be informed by labour market demands for highly skilled workforces and the reduced demand for manual labour. The latter are informed by subsistence, largely agricultural, economies. What constitutes childhood and its attendant policies is variable.

Historians have also viewed childhood as something of a 'moveable feast', with some commentators seeing childhood as a relatively recent phenomenon with its roots in the seventeenth century and an increased separation of children from adults, especially in public life (Aries 1962). While this may have been the case for children of the aristocracy and the emerging trading classes, working-class children were entering the adult labour force and working alongside their parents from an early age. Stone (1977) sees class position as an important factor in the constitution of childhood, with perceptions of childhood vulnerability growing in the nineteenth century as the 'upper and middle classes . . . had . . . more time to devote to child care concerns' (Corby 1993: 10). MacFarlane (1979) has dismissed this materialist view, arguing that childhood is not merely the product of changing economic conditions. Corby concludes that more recent historical evidence suggests that the concept of childhood has always existed:

> although there is no doubt that children in former times were expected to work and become what we today would consider to be adult at an earlier age than our own children . . . It seems likely that children have always had a separate status, particularly early on when they are physically dependent. As societies develop economically there is a tendency for childhood to be extended and to gain more attention as

a separate category, a process that is testified to by the growth of child protective legislation.

(Corby 1993: 11)

The late twentieth century saw an extension of childhood as a separate category and the constitution of children as vulnerable and in need of protection. The legislative removal of under-16s from the labour market has extended both their dependency on adults and their vulnerability.

Debates about the 'discovery' of child abuse have been just as contentious (Corby 1993). The lack of historical evidence, interpretations of historical accounts and the differing notions of acceptable parenting and childcare have hampered analysis in differing historical periods. The weight of historical evidence suggests that all eras have been concerned with the appropriate care and nurture of children, and that while 'every generation needs to think it is improving on the past', the identification and regulation of child abuse have been a perennial issue (Corby 1993: 15). What is subject to change, however, is how child abuse is defined and regulated.

In his analysis of state and voluntary sector responses to child abuse from 1870 to the 1989 Children Act, Corby demonstrates the 'ambivalence and uncertainty' of policy responses, oscillating uneasily between intervention and regulation of families on the one hand, and desires to preserve the independence of family life on the other. The immediate post-Second World War period was characterized by a 'welfarist' approach to child abuse, with local committees empowered to oversee 'problem families' (Home Office 1950), and the subsequent 1952 Children and Young Persons Act (Amendment) gave local children's departments child protection powers. Social case work with families tended towards prevention and the avoidance of receptions into care, with casework interventions influenced by the theories of Bowlby (1951) on loss and 'maternal deprivation'. Problem families were associated with 'cycles of deprivation', and child abuse was medicalized as the 'battered baby syndrome' (Kempe et al. 1962; Okell and Butcher 1969). Support and the welfarist 'policing' of families (Donzelot 1980) continued to dominate child abuse throughout the 1960s, with the 1969 Children and Young Persons Act making neglect, 'failure to thrive' and delinquency grounds for social work interventions into family life. This approach was influenced by the American work of Kempe et al. (1962), which sought both to medicalize the 'battered baby syndrome' and to identify those families in need of help and support. The 1968 Seebohm Committee that proposed a generalist, family-oriented social work service paralleled this. Seebohm was implemented in 1971.

Social work in this period has been characterized as a form of social engineering within the broader framework of a welfarist driven social policy (Rose and Miller 1992; Parton 1994). Interventions were largely benign and optimistic, with the scientific–medical approach to social casework enjoying both consensus and confidence. The 1970s saw a growing challenge to both this consensus and optimism. The tide turned with the death and subsequent public inquiry into the death of Maria Colwell (Parton 1979), and the extensive media coverage and vilification of the social work profession that followed. As Cochrane (1993: 82) puts it, 'The 1980s was a decade of inquiries into and reports on the many aspects of social work practice which helped to create a beleaguered context for the profession.' Eighteen child death inquiries followed in which the lack of vigilance and intervention of social workers was repeatedly highlighted (Saraga 1993). The inquiries introduced two key themes into the arena of social work with children: increased accountability and regulation through public inquiries and the Social Services Inspectorate, and a judicial scrutiny of rights, responsibilities and procedures. The subsequent Department of Health (1991b) review of the inquiries attempted to draw broad lessons from the varied conclusions of the individual reports. However, given the nature of the original reports this proved difficult, and left the Department to conclude that:

> a key issue needs to be addressed further. That is the relationship between policies, procedures and practices of individual agencies in relation to child protection and how these relate to the law, in particular to the statutory duties of the local authority and the most effective way in which agencies can work together.
>
> (Department of Health 1991b: 110)

The subsequent document, *Working Together* (Home Office *et al.* 1991), emphasized increased accountability and partnership. The 1990s saw a significant increase in proceduralization, rules, codes of practice and formalized assessments for child protection work (Hallett and Birchall 1992; Kemshall *et al.* 1997). These developments have shifted attention from children and families 'in need' to children 'at risk' and requiring protection; hence the new terminology of child protection rather than the language of child abuse prevention (DHSS 1988; Kemshall *et al.* 1997; Parton *et al.* 1997). The 1989 Children Act established evidence, procedures and criteria as essential to appropriate decision-making in child protection. While support for families and the 'welfare of the child' were emphasized, the criterion for social work intervention was established through para. 31(2)(a): 'that the child concerned is suffering, or is likely to suffer significant harm'. As Parton *et al.* claim that this established the risk of harm, its accurate prediction and the need to establish thresholds of harm as essential to the practice of child protection. It also firmly established children as an 'at-risk' group, vulnerable to harmful risks and in need of state protection via social work services.

Jackson and Scott (1999: 86) argue that children are constructed as a 'protected species and childhood as a protected state' and as such both are a site for 'risk anxiety'. Sexual risks to children and moral panics over paedophiles are a clear example of such anxiety (Kitzinger 1999). Paedophilic threat to childhood innocence is particularly feared, and results in exaggerated perceptions of risk (Kemshall 1999). Not only is innocence a key component of such a constitution of risk, so is vulnerability and the 'specialness' of childhood (as distinct from adulthood). Jackson and Scott argue that the peculiar risk anxiety of childhood is engendered by public scepticism of professional and expert knowledge and competence to manage risk. This is exacerbated by Giddens's 'existential angst', in which the general unpredictability of the social world produces almost daily anxiety (Giddens 1990, 1991). The shadowy paedophile in our midst is all-pervasive, engendering parental and societal anxiety that is rarely alleviated by public policy responses. The individualization of risk articulated by Giddens literally leaves each parent individually to calculate and manage risks for their own children. This position is exacerbated by the destabilization endemic in late modernity, the fracturing of traditional bonds of place, class and gender resulting in a 'climate of fear' and a 'worship of safety' (Furedi 1997). Current constructions and responses to childhood risks are a clear illustration of late modernity's preoccupation with risk. The locus of this risk in the 'stranger-danger' of the 'Other' is not coincidental. Paedophile risk is the most highly rated risk to children, albeit out of proportion to recorded risks to children from paedophiles (Kitzinger 1999) and disproportionate to the rate of sexual abuse suffered by children from known adults in their own home (Wyre 1997). However, what parent could afford to act 'rationally' on such information? The perceived terror that it 'could be your child' far outweighs any 'objective' or 'rational' calculation of actual risks. The need to keep children safe also extends their dependency and distinctiveness from adults (Jackson 1982; Jackson and Scott 1999), and functions both to regulate childhood (acceptable behaviours and attitudes, for example) and to regulate family life (Donzelot 1980). Responsibility for such regulation has been increasingly displaced from the state to individual parents; a key mechanism of individual regulation within advanced liberal societies.

Drawing on Foucault's theory of power, Moss *et al.* (2000) contend that the notion of the 'child in need' and the 'child at risk' is constructed through the dominant discourse of modernity's welfarist normalization of families. This locates children in a bounded space within which certain behaviours, activities and attitudes are seen as normal or deviant. They argue that this discourse has located childhood in the private domain and as individualized and dependent. State intervention and regulation of the private domain of family life is then rationalized by the discourse of need, and more recently through the discourse of risk and vulnerability, particularly for those families seen as dysfunctional and as the locus of social problems and disorder. The emphasis is increasingly upon 'changing parental behaviour' to tackle both childhood delinquency and social discipline (Jordan 2000). The Children Act 1989 is an example of this delicate balance between the privacy and autonomy of families, and the need to discipline and regulate 'problem families'.

The 'elderly' have also been constituted as a group in need of social work services, and presented as high users of both health care and personal social services even where this runs contrary to the current evidence on levels of use (Littlechild and Glasby 2000). Townsend (1993: 223) has argued that 'the material and psychological dependence of older people' has been produced by the late twentieth-century social policy response to post-Fordist patterns of production. In brief, these changing patterns have resulted in rapid changes in skills and knowledge, and in the multinational dispersal of productivity to the Third World. From the 1970s onwards this has resulted in the displacement of older workers and an increased stratification of the workforce by age. In essence, Townsend argues that retirement has operated as a form of mass redundancy. This enforced dependency has been compounded by the low rate of income from pensions and state benefits, particularly in relation to the rest of the working (and younger) population. State pensions in particular have failed to maintain the income level of pensioners, and the increased emphasis upon private provision has not always been universally welcomed (Brindle 1996). Other assets tend to depreciate, or are subject to means testing in order to achieve care services. In this process both financial and physical independence are eroded by the structure of state provision.

While current views tend to present the marginalization and dependency of older persons as a peculiarly twentieth-century phenomenon, Johnson (1998a) argues that historical evidence is less clear cut. Despite partial historical evidence, he concludes that functional and physical capacity have long been a key determinant in attitudes to old age, particularly functionality in economic or military terms. Ability and function determined the kinds of rights, inclusion and participation that older persons enjoyed, and this illustrates how underlying economic and social pressures condition attitudes and behaviour towards old age. However, Johnson does contend that 'the transition from retirement as an exceptional circumstance to retirement as a social norm' is a peculiarly twentieth-century phenomenon. This expansion has gone from a very few in the Victorian age to half the workforce in occupational pensions by the close of the twentieth century, with virtually everyone entitled to state provision (Johnson 1998b). The extent to which this is a welcome development is of course dependent upon both individual resources to enjoy retirement and the state's collective resources to fund a continually expanding demand. However, despite massive expansion in pension provision, poverty in old age remains a perennial issue (Johnson 1998b). Johnson locates retirement and pensions legislation within an overall trend informed by modernization and the 'logic of industrialism', in which compulsory retirement is a response to the 'functional redundancy of older workers brought about by the technological imperatives of industrialisation' (p. 213).

While the initial pension legislation was based upon an insurance scheme, politicians were acutely aware that they could not give pensioners a 'blank cheque' (p. 215). By the inception of the welfare state, Beveridge was concerned with the 'very high cost involved in providing them all with a pension income' (Beveridge 1942: 90). From the very beginning pensions were linked with the demands of the labour market and economic considerations. Both continued to dominate the development of pensions policy and with it the nature of retirement and perceptions of old age throughout the twentieth century.

Community and residential care also play their part in fostering dependency (Townsend 1993; Hugman 1994). Residential care creates and maintains enforced dependency, with the processes of institutionalization fostering passivity and deindividualizing residents. However, as Townsend states, the 'number of bedfast, severely incapacitated and infirm old people living in the community dwarfs the number in institutions' (p. 225). This is not reflected in either community care services or the allocation of resources between residential and community provision. As Townsend puts it, priorities have yet to change. Where community care does exist, it is often created in the image of the dominant residential sector, with day care centres, for example, following the familiar organizational and institutional pattern of care homes. Social work with the elderly has often been characterized as less skilful and has compounded ageism and discrimination against older persons as service users with needs subordinated to resources and increased segregation in service delivery (Hugman 1994). The framing of 'care of the elderly' is in terms of minimum 'top-up' for those who cannot self-care or self-manage. This is in sharp contrast to the 'optimal care' as a needs-led right proposed by Doyal (1993). Assessments are framed by the language of compensation and failure, what is required to compensate for the failure of the older person's family or social network to cope, or to compensate for the failure to self-care.

However, as Littlechild and Blakeney (1996: 69) point out:

> The vast majority of older people in Britain live in their own homes and make arrangements for any necessary care with no recourse to formal sources of help. The 1985 Household survey indicated that 75 per cent of people aged 75 and over received no help at all from Social Services or domiciliary health services.

It is only when such arrangements break down that they 'come under the scrutiny of helping professionals' (Littlechild and Blakeney 1996: 69). The issue of risk arises when admission into residential care has to be considered or when supporting networks of care breakdown (Kemshall et al. 1997). However, as Herring and Thom (1997: 234) put it, 'the image of the frail, vulnerable older person is a powerful one', and influences both public and policy views of older persons. This powerful stereotype has been used to patronize and increase the dependency of older persons, and to undermine their capacity to make choices (Norman 1980). Choice, a central principle of community care, can be significantly undermined by professional desires to prevent risk. As the next section argues, the assessments that professionals make are increasingly framed by notions of vulnerability and risk rather than by need.

Summary

The period between the implementation of Seebohm in 1971 and the implementation of the National Health Service and Community Care Act 1990 saw unprecedented change in the role, responsibilities and structure of the personal social services. Most notable was the increased fiscal and practice control, coupled with a purchaser–provider split, and the reconstitution of social work departments as coordinating purchasers of community care. Social policy trends since the inception of the welfare state have contributed to the framing of both children and the elderly as dependent groups in need of compensatory provision. Meeting such need has become increasingly problematic as costs have spiralled, and welfarist social engineering has given way to a 'new welfare consensus' in which targeting and gatekeeping through tightly controlled assessment is the key. Such assessments are increasingly framed by concepts of risk and vulnerability rather than by need.

The personal social services: needs-led or risk-led?

The Community Care Act redefined care services, and the subsequent guidance placed an obligation on local authorities to 'assess people's needs holistically in relation to a wide range of possible service options, rather than having separate service-led assessments' (Department of Health 1991c). In theory this should have promoted tailor-made services to meet highly individualized assessments of need, and need should outweigh notions of eligibility in service delivery (Browne 1996). Care packages or care plans were to form the central plank of service provision and service-led provision was to be replaced by needs-led provision. The Department of Health (1991c) guidance stressed needs-based assessment, collaboration between workers, clients and their carers and cost-effectiveness. The statement from the Secretary of State, *Caring for People* (1989), also emphasized the promotion of care plans to enable people to remain in their own homes. These inherent tensions between choice, user empowerment, cost-effectiveness and the avoidance of costly residential care have plagued community care provision since its inception (Ellis 1993). Ellis *et al.* (1999: 266) point out that *Caring for People* set contradictory objectives for local authorities, requiring needs-led services and greater consumer choice but targeting resources 'only on the most needy'. This tension was exacerbated by lack of resources for community care. 'Need' is notorious for its ability to outstrip supply (Baldock 1994; Ellis *et al.* 1999). The inherent difficulty of meeting the 'expressed need' of users (Bradshaw 1972) was recognized by the subsequent guidance issued by the Department of Health, in which the necessity of 'difficult decisions' was recognized: 'difficult decisions . . . will be necessary to strike a balance between meeting the needs identified within available resources and meeting the care preferences of the individual' (Department of Health 1990a: para. 3.25).

The community care changes were also aimed at redefining the practice of social workers away from 'self-serving' bureaucracy and costly professional discretion to a more top-down, managerially controlled delivery of care. This has been achieved through fiscal control and increased regulation of practice, coupled with the eradication of professional power and autonomy (Newman and Clarke 1994). Fiscal control in particular was seen as a key mechanism in the control of runaway spending on nursing home and residential care (Lewis and Glennerster 1996). Fiscal control has been paralleled by practice guidance (Department of Health 1991d, e) and an increased use of audit to promote practice control and accountability (Power 1994). The monitoring role and function of the Audit Commission, Social Services Inspectorate and regional health authorities has grown accordingly. Managerialism has replaced professional discretion in the delivery of social care:

> A raft of disciplinary measures, such as performance indicators, cost centres, customer surveys, staff appraisal systems and performance-related pay, were imposed to ensure attitudinal and behavioural compliance among frontline staff.
> (Newman and Clarke 1994: 20; cited in Ellis *et al.* 1999: 267–8)

While transforming social services departments from providers to purchasers and relocating 'purchasing decisions as close to the consumer as possible' was presented as an enhancement of consumer choice and user empowerment (Ellis *et al.* 1999: 268), such devolved care management was in effect a technique for controlling 'run away spend' on expensive forms of care provision. As Ellis *et al.* (1999: 268) argue, the purchaser–provider split separates 'the assessment of need from the provision of services'. The role for social workers has changed from long-term interventions to heavily prescribed assessment and case management in which 'needs talk' and 'services talk' do not necessarily add up (Cheetham 1993). Social work tasks increasingly came to have an administrative and technical character rather than a professional one (Lawson 1993; Ellis *et al.* 1999). For Jordan (2000) this has resulted in an 'arm's length service', with social workers removed from the street and largely engaged in the top-down social engineering of New Labour.

Eliminating need: the rise of vulnerability

The personal social services as created by Seebohm had promised responsivity to local need and provision to children, families, individuals and communities 'in need'. However, such open-ended commitment came with a price, potentially unlimited demand and spiralling costs. Local social services departments responded to such pressure through rationing, either bureaucratically reducing services or imposing restrictive rules of eligibility (Smith 1980; Foster 1983). By the 1980s reconciling the 'expressed need' of clients with the provision actually available was a perennial problem (Bradshaw 1972, 1994; Smith 1980; Kemshall 1984). Difficult rationing decisions were often hidden from public view by the delegation of such decision-making to front-line staff. This resulted in various practitioner tactics such as 'people processing', in which clients were dealt with merely administratively (Hill 1969), or through techniques such as 'street-level bureaucracy' (Lipsky 1980), in which workers bend agency rules in order to survive the high pressure of unmeetable demand. The New Right control of welfare and social spend demanded both tighter gatekeeping of provision and a more circumspect definition of need. In effect, the 1980s saw the expressed need of clients replaced by the managerially defined need of funders and purchasers. As Ellis *et al.* (1999: 269) put it, 'Despite the rhetoric of needs-based assessments, the concept of need was indistinguishable from criteria defining eligibility for services.'

Eligibility became inextricably caught up with rationing, formal or otherwise. The Audit Commission (1992: 31) advised that eligible needs should be defined according to priorities. Such prioritization necessitated gatekeeping and targeting, controlling access to services through the very process of assessment itself. Assessment became concerned with the identification of those most vulnerable and for whom costly residential care could be avoided if community services were appropriately targeted (Challis 1992). Assessment itself became a major tool of rationing access and defining eligibility under the Community Care Act (Ellis *et al.* 1999). Needs-led assessment was no longer driven by the expressed need of clients, or the professional judgement of workers, but by the top-down managerially defined priorities of local authorities. Gatekeeping was considerably simplified by replacing the inclusive and ambiguous concept of need with the exclusive and managerially defined concept of 'vulnerability', in which clearer priorities could be set.

This is reflected in applications for local authority residential care, in which vulnerability is a key feature. Neill *et al.* (1988) found that out of a thousand such applications four-fifths identified the older person as being 'at risk', and nine out of ten referrals for residential care identified risk as an important factor in decisions about service delivery. The Department of Health (1991e: 59) practitioner guidance on assessment and care management acknowledges the importance of risk assessment, but recognizes that agencies and workers will 'vary in their perceptions of risk and crisis'. Some workers will perceive risk to independence as greater than risks to physical well-being, for example. The Community Care Act has also led to an increase in assessments of older people prior to discharge from hospital, in which workers are again confronted by conflicting risks and competing tensions between speedy through-put of patients and safe discharge (Little-child and Blakeney 1996). Vulnerability and being 'at risk' provides access to either residential or hospital care and alternative or subsequent services in the community.

The NHS Community Care Act enshrined the notion of individual choice and non-residential care as central principles (Griffiths 1988; Herring and Thom 1997). Isaacs and Evers (1981) have argued that risk is essential to the exercise of such choice, and that community as opposed to residential care embodies the notion of acceptable risk. In an era of increased litigation and accountability for risk decisions (Carson 1996) it is perhaps not surprising that the subsequent development of community care has resulted in a growing emphasis upon formalized risk policies and frameworks for the assessment of risk (Lawson 1996). The Social Services Inspectorate (1993: 21) attempted to capture this delicate balance:

> Exercising choice and control involves risks, and independence should not be unnecessarily curtailed because of others' fears. Restrictions of rights and freedoms should be strictly limited, subject to agreed safe-guards. Agencies should have clear written policies on risk taking.

In effect, the tricky job of balancing risks and rights is devolved to local authority social services departments.

Eliminating need: the rise of child protection

The Seebohm reorganization of personal social services promised much in terms of the care of children and families. However, the 1980s saw the social services under almost perpetual challenge. The decade opened with Brewer and Lait (1980) posing the famous question: 'Can social work survive?' A series of child death inquiries added to the general perception of a profession under siege and social work departments and their employees became familiar with the concept of blame (Reder *et al.* 1993). However, if the NHS Community Care Act salvaged some vestige of adult services for the personal social services, the 1989 Children Act provided a continued role for social workers in their work with children. The Act provided 'a new legislative framework and a clearer definition of the role of social work in child protection' (Langan 1993: 153).

Langan (1993: 154) argues that three important factors influenced the formulation of the Children Act:

- the growth of compulsory receptions into care from the 1970s onwards;
- the rediscovery of child abuse in the 1980s, the increase in child death inquiries and increased calls for a more interventionist stance towards families and children 'at risk';
- the over-intrusion reported by the Cleveland inquiry and the subsequent calls for a more judicial and evidential approach to child abuse investigations.

Cleveland in particular demonstrated the need to 'reconcile the tension between family autonomy and state intervention' (Langan 1993: 154). The 1989 Children Act transformed the nature of social work with children and families by:

- Providing a juridical framework for intervention that emphasized social workers' accountability to the courts. Parton (1991) has argued that this transformed the definition of child abuse from the socio-medical sphere to the socio-legal definition of child protection.
- Assessment was made central to all investigations and subsequent work, and in effect constituted social services departments as the lead agency. Parton (1991: 146) has argued that 'social knowledge' is central to such assessments and is the key mechanism for identifying high-risk cases.
- Establishing a threshold of high risk through the use of 'significant harm' and setting this as the criterion 'for invoking the statutory powers of the new 'emergency protection' or 'child assessment' order (Langan 1993: 155). Social workers must now distinguish between high-risk and other cases and only intervene in the former. The welfare of the child is paramount.
- Preventative action is justified for those children and families 'in need', usually provided by referring to other (sometimes voluntary) agencies (from Langan 1993: 155–6).

While the Act attempts to balance intervention and prevention, in reality intervention is enforced by statutory powers, while preventative work remains discretionary. Langan (1992) forecast that this would result in an almost exclusive focus on statutory work at the expense of preventative provision, and this has indeed been the result as evidenced by the Audit Commission (1994a) report *Seen but Not Heard*. Drawing on a number of empirical and statistical sources Parton *et al.* (1997) argue that the number of children on registers has quadrupled between 1978 and 1991. They also contend that this figure belies the actual number of investigations and particularly those investigations of allegations of child abuse which do not result in any further action. The trend towards investigations rather than prevention and the juridical emphasis upon forensic evidence in particular has resulted in a reframing of social work with children in term of risk and protection. Douglas (1992) and others (Kemshall *et al.* 1997) have argued that risk lends itself particularly well to such forensic functions, to investigations of what went wrong and to blame allocation – whether that be failing social workers, failing procedures or failing families. In addition to blame allocation, risk also lends itself to resource allocation, facilitating 'targeting matrices' and eligibility thresholds based upon risk of harm criteria (Kemshall 1998). Accountability to set procedures, assessment tools and 'defensible decisions' is also enhanced (Carson 1996; Kemshall 1998).

These trends are evident in official guidance, such as DHSS (1988), Department of Health (1988, 1991f), Home Office *et al.* (1991) and Directors of Social Work in Scotland (1992). These documents not only established child protection as a specialist area of social work practice, but also established it as part of a wider inter-agency net governed by evidential principles and heavy proceduralization. The interviewing of children, for example, is governed by rules of evidence and the law (Department of Health and Home Office 1992a: 2–3). Langan (1993: 97) concludes that in this context 'Notions of treatment and therapy become less important as general bases of intervention: instead the language is that of protection and of managing cases or managing risk'. As Kemshall *et al.* (1997: 214) put it:

> It is our hypothesis . . . that as issues concerned with responsibility, accountability and rationing come to the fore, so do concerns with risk. As this happens, even the language of need itself will become couched and differentiated in terms of risk. Notions of risk are taking central significance in characterising the emerging rationality and rationale for organising the personal social services.

Summary

Community care assessment, while rhetorically enshrining the principles of choice and individual need, has in reality been dominated by resource control and rationing. 'Needs talk' and 'services talk' have been increasingly difficult to reconcile. Eligibility rules and threshold criteria have become central to service delivery in the personal social services, and such rules and criteria have increasingly been reframed by official guidance, policy documents and local practice in terms of vulnerability and risk, rather than need. In terms of 'care of the elderly', risk has become both a mechanism by which to access scarce and costly resources such as residential care, and a site of potential conflict between users and workers. Workers assess risk not only to determine eligibility for services, but also to prevent harm to users and to avoid potentially costly and damaging litigation. In the sphere of 'child-care', work with children and families is increasingly determined by issues of risk reduction and child protection rather than prevention and the amelioration of need. In this sphere risk is not only an important mechanism for the management of cases, it also provides a useful tool in the forensic investigation of allegations, proceduralization of investigations and account-ability of workers to managerially desirable outcomes.

Risk assessment and risk management in the personal social services

The 1990s saw an increasing preoccupation with risk in the policies and practices of the personal social services (Feaviour *et al*. 1995; Department of Health 1999a, b). Risk has become a central feature of the practice of both managers and workers in all aspects of social care (Kemshall and Pritchard 1996), and is embedded in many of the features and procedures of organizational life (Kemshall *et al*. 1997). The identification of risk and the categorization of risk into thresholds for intervention and service delivery have become key mechanisms in the rationing of scarce social care resources. Kemshall *et al*. identify two significant indicators of the shift to risk:

- the use of risk as a monitoring tool and as a mechanism for accountability;
- the use of risk as a rationing device and case prioritizing tool.

The 'Risk Initiative' by the Social Services Inspectorate in 1995 is seen as a significant watershed in the introduction of risk concerns to social service policies and procedures. The document identifies a range of risks for concern: risks to service users, carers and care workers, managers and agencies. The Inspectorate in effect set a number of 'risk standards' for use in inspections, summarized as:

- whether senior managers ensure that there are policies, procedures and guidance on risk issues, that these are understood and followed by staff or the social services department and other service providers, and that they are regularly reviewed;
- that risks are analysed and appropriately managed at all stages of the referral, assessment and care management process;
- that the suitability of prospective staff members (and other people provid-ing care such as foster parents) is thoroughly checked before appointment, and when staff are in post they receive appropriate guidance, training and support to enable them to perform tasks with awareness and understand-ing of the possible risk issues;
- that senior staff and care workers receive appropriate equipment, guidance, training and support in relation to issues of health, safety and security of users, staff and premises (from Kemshall *et al*. 1997: 215).

In effect, the SSI document not only requires social services departments to manage risk, but also to manage service delivery *by* risk, that is, to use risk as a principle of resource allocation and case management.

Monitoring and accountability

Douglas has demonstrated that the contemporary use of the term risk is as a 'forensic' resource, a mechanism for investigating what has gone wrong and for the allocation of blame and liability (Douglas 1992: 27). For Douglas the use and application of the term risk indicates the type of blaming system operating: 'the one we are in now is almost ready to treat every death as chargeable to someone's account, every accident as caused by someone's criminal negligence, every sickness a threatened prosecution' (Douglas 1992: 15–16). In other words, someone must be held accountable (Kemshall et al. 1997). Risk has a forensic function in the personal social services, in which the avoidance of litigation and blame has become the central feature (Carson 1996). Not only do workers risk 'legal repercussions', they also risk vilification and public blame. The 'risk society' has not only emphasized risks, but also eroded public trust in professionals who work with risk and in the institutions they represent (Giddens 1994). Giddens sees trust and risk as inextricably linked: 'What is seen as an "acceptable" risk – the minimising of danger – varies in different contexts, but is usually central in sustaining trust' (Giddens 1990: 35).

Trust is essential to the maintenance of confidence and credibility in expert knowledge systems; for example, social work and its constituent parts, such as child protection. Where such trust is fractured – for example, by lapses in expert knowledge and systems to regulate the risk effectively – media and public demands for increased formalized accountability quickly follow. The regulation of child protection from the 1970s onwards exemplifies this. The 1989 Children Act, for example, represents a legislative attempt to bring child protection work under control and to introduce greater accountability through judicial processes. The Community Care Act and subsequent documents also introduced prescriptive guidance for practice and accountability systems. Formalized systems of management and accountability are now well embedded in the operation of the personal social services (Clarke et al. 1994). Audit has become an essential mechanism for holding practitioners to account and for eradicating the inherent uncertainties of social work. Such audits have replaced trust, thereby reducing the autonomy and professional status of workers. Such audits:

> increasingly use notions of risk in order to judge the quality of the practices being investigated, whether this is of the individual case or more generally in the organisational processes of welfare agencies themselves. Notions of risk are becoming increasingly endemic in an organisational culture that needs a common forensic vocabulary with which to hold individuals accountable, and to allocate scarce resources.
>
> (Kemshall et al. 1997: 224)

The move to audit and accountability has been particularly acute in social work, not least because the nature of social work is characterized by high degrees of uncertainty and ambiguity. Reliable predictions are unlikely, and many risk assessments are highly individualized. In these circumstances probabilistic reasoning is difficult, and risk assessments are characterized by a number of 'it depends' and uncertainty about desirable outcomes. Regulating risk in these circumstances is characterized by a 'lifeboat' or 'anticipatory' approach in which risk assessors attempt to calculate and prepare for a range of 'it depends' and seek to maintain a flexible attitude to alternative possibilities (Wildavsky 1988). This approach can, however, make managers removed from front-line assessment highly anxious about the quality and efficacy of such decisions (Kemshall 1998). This can result in contradictory practice guidance in which workers are advised to exercise case-by-case judgement while also following highly prescriptive procedures (Her Majesty's Inspectorate of Probation 1997; Lawrie 1997). Such procedures can add to the uncertainty of both practitioners and managers by failing to provide practitioners with a risk assessment tool. Procedures exhort workers to take particular actions but do not enable them to assess risk (Kemshall 1998).

In a climate of uncertainty, organizational responses to risk failures tend to be in terms of blame (Hood *et al.* 1992). Emphasis is then placed upon documentation of risk, step-by-step procedures that can be audited and the creation of processes that can demonstrate 'defensibility' and withstand hindsight scrutiny in the light of things going wrong. This approach is resource-intensive and results in an over-emphasis upon identification and assessment at the cost of management and intervention. In child protection for example this has resulted in a pre-occupation with investigations at the expense of prevention (Parton *et al.* 1997). In such settings the 'precautionary principle' of better safe than sorry tends to widen the net and strain resources. While blame is often advocated as a mechanism for preventing recurrence, in reality this is rarely achieved (Horlick-Jones 1996). Its major function is to allocate blame away from the corporate centre to the individual practitioner, and to provide an instance of 'ritual damnation': 'Find someone to blame, cries the mob, and off runs Whitehall to offer up someone to blame' (Jenkins 1998).

Risk, rationing and case prioritization

The 1989 Children Act placed an obligation on local authorities to 'safeguard and promote the welfare of children within their area who are in need' (section 17(1)). However, as Colton *et al.* (1995) have argued, 'children in need' is so inadequately defined by the Act that its implementation is hampered. While section 17(10) offers three definitions of 'children in need', the terminology used is itself open to ambiguity and interpretation;

for example, 'reasonable standard of health and development' and 'significantly impaired'. In essence, this has left social services departments with significant discretion in defining both need and service provision. Within a climate of scarce resources and in the absence of guidance, this left the social workers in Colton *et al.*'s study to 'make decisions on the basis of their own personal, and differing, interpretations of the meaning of "need"' (Colton *et al.* 1995: 715).

In effect, the workers applied specific categories of need: children who were at risk of abuse or neglect and children who were disabled. The obligation to identify the extent to which children are in need in their geographic area (Schedule 2) was similarly implemented, with the emphasis upon risk of abuse and neglect and the identification of children with disabilities. Children in need were ranked in terms of priority for services, and this ranking confirmed that children at risk of abuse and neglect were seen as the major priority, with sexual abuse having an average priority ranking of 1.5 and poverty 7.81. In an overall ranking of nine factors sexual abuse is at the top, with poverty last. While managers recognized the desirability of weighing all needs equally, in effect scarce resources resulted in the prioritization of child protection cases above other cases and within child protection, ranking cases according to the severity of risk and the likely harm. In a similar study Aldgate *et al.* (1992) also concluded that most of the resources under the 1989 Act would go to child protection, with insufficient resources left for prevention.

Colton *et al.* identify the key tension in the 1989 Act: the definitions of need within the Act may intend wide-ranging provision, but the implementation of the Act has to take place within a political climate of residualism in welfare. They define this as collectivist in theory but residualist in practice: 'The "collectivist" philosophy manifested in the Children Act cannot be easily put into practice in a "residualist" society' (Colton *et al.* 1995: 727).

Service provision to older people, while collectivist in spirit, has also become residualist in reality. Need has increasingly been prioritized, with those 'in need' transformed into those most vulnerable and 'at risk' if services are not provided. This has resulted in highly 'selective assessment':

Where services are provided on the basis of the principle of universality, such as National Insurance retirement pensions, only enough assessment is required to confirm that a person falls within an impersonal category. But where provision is organised on the principle of selectivity, as in the health and personal welfare sectors, more complex assessment is required in order both to ration (target) resources, and to link correctly any applicant to what is available.

(Key 1989: 68)

Despite Key's arguments for 'affirmative assessment', in which both uniqueness and equality of opportunity are stressed, selective assessment is open to managerial steer via practice guidance, resource constraint and decisions of pragmatism and expediency, and political boundaries such as residualism. Such real constraints may run contrary to the expressed needs of elders, resulting in functional assessments of 'objective requirements' such as minimal assistance with physical care, rather than affirmative assessments of the levels of care required for dignity or quality of life. Rights as well as needs can be denied, especially in those circumstances where workers and their agencies will not 'run the risk' (Kemshall and Pritchard 1997). Provision such as compulsory care is then used for those deemed in need of care and attention (Norman 1980), thus threatening independence (*Community Care* 1995).

Hospital social workers are often required to make 'snap decisions' about both admission and discharge (*Community Care* 1996), leading to a 'vicious circle that leads to the increasing use of acute hospital beds by older people' (Littlechild and Glasby 2000: 145; see also Audit Commission 1997). This compounds their perceived vulnerability and adds to professional and public perceptions about their overuse and unnecessary use of health care beds. Littlechild and Glasby's study, in which admissions were found to be for medical and not social reasons, challenges this misperception, and suggests that discharge was hampered by the inadequate provision of rehabilitative services.

This ambivalent attitude to provision for older persons is long-standing and is well captured in the 1947 Rowntree Report on ageing:

> In recent years there has been a considerable awakening of public interest in the problems of old age, an awakening that has manifested itself in a sympathetic attitude to old people and in a widespread desire to be generous to them. The Committee are in full sympathy with this attitude but they have felt bound to take into account another point of view, based not on any lack of sympathy with the aged but on a recognition of the country's strictly limited resources of wealth and labour, and the rapidly growing proportion of old people in the total population.
>
> (Rowntree 1947: 95)

In the following 50 years this alternative view has become more acute, such that the 'Millennium debate of the age' was on ageing (Age Concern 2000). With 20 per cent of the UK population over 60, and with the post-Second World War generation fast approaching retirement, adequate pensioner incomes and 'care of the elderly' have attracted both media coverage and political attention. The generation that created and paid for the welfare state is now confronted with low pay-outs and selective provision, a situation which attracts protest and with one-third of the electorate over 55 potential electoral disaster for political parties that fail to take the 'grey vote' seriously (BBC 2000a). As Hargreaves and Christie (1998: 40) put it, the twentieth century became the 'age of age'. However, the changing pattern of life has itself radically challenged the concept of age. Hargreaves and Christie (1998: 42) highlight the difficulty in continuing to use the retirement age as a proxy for need, a crude mechanism for providing universal provision for the 'infirm' above a particular age:

> the age of 60 or 65 no longer seems a good proxy for need. Surveys suggest that although there are some near-universal needs among the retired – for instance, 97 per cent of over-65s need glasses or contact lenses – there is a large proportion of reasonably healthy, active and mobile pensioners. Over-65s make only two visits more to their doctor on average each year than do sixteen to 44 year-olds. And only about two out of every five pensioners report having any sort of disability. Far fewer are actually registered as disabled.

They argue that this can only result in misplaced spending at a level too large to ignore. The lessening of working years to support the growing number of retirement years exacerbates this problem. The outcome is over-spending on healthy, relatively well-off pensioners at the expense of the infirm, and despite 'half the welfare budget' being spent on aged-based pensions, a recent Department of Social Security report on poverty highlighted an increase in the number of pensioners living in poverty, with up to 100,000 people affected in 1998–9 (BBC 2000b). Hargreaves and Christie (1998: 44) argue for a massive redistribution of resources from the basis of age to dis-ability and infirmity, which would enable 'more to be given to the poor, sick and disabled elderly who need the money most'. Such a transition neces-sitates acceptance of working beyond present age limits and the 'decent citizen saving for their retirement' (Field 2000). This is the self-regulation of risk promulgated by the Third Way. As Jordan (2000) puts it, the collec-tivist ideas of community are grafted on to the economic imperatives of neo-liberalism.

Conclusions

The personal social services have become increasingly residualized and con-cerned predominantly with those excluded from the labour market and thus outside the positive social engineering of the Third Way. 'Bad' welfare spend has been reduced, and 'DIY welfare' has become the norm. As the principle of universal provision has been displaced by selective provision and the assess-ment systems which accompany it, the social work discourse of need has been replaced by a pragmatic and largely managerially defined language of risk. The transition is by no means wholesale, but is evidenced by the use of risk to ration and target resources, to monitor case management and to hold staff to account. In work with children and families 'protection' from risk and harm predominates, in work with older persons 'vulnerability' and protection from risks are central to many of the decisions made by front-line workers. This trend can be viewed as part of a larger 'economic rationalist' approach to welfare risks, in which risk-based targeting of benefits is a central feature (Simon 1987). Welfare spend is in effect descaled by this risk-based discourse. O'Malley (1992), however, sees it as a wider form of prudentialism; that is, a redistribution of risk management from the social and state sphere to the individual and the use of increasingly disciplinary techniques to regularize behaviour. A key factor in this transition has been the New Right assertion that social insurance cannot necessarily guarantee the efficiency of the economy or regularize conflicts between different areas of the market economy (Gough 1984). Only privatized arrangements can revitalize both the individual and society from the complacency and 'perverse incentives' of the welfare state (Gamble 1988). As O'Malley (1992: 261) puts it,

> Better understood as prudentialism, it is a construct of governance that removes the key conception of regulating individuals by collectivist risk management, and throws back upon the individual the responsibility for managing risk. This may be advocated by supporters as 'efficient', for individuals will be driven to greater exertion and enterprise by the need to insure against adverse circumstances – and the more enterprising they are, the better the safety net they can construct.

Such prudentialism is the hallmark of the decent citizen. Where prudentialism has not been efficiently effected or has failed, the state's residual safety net will step in; hence the targeting of the 'very old', the 'frail elderly' and the 'poor elderly'. For those of us yet to approach old age, prudential provision is urged upon us and we are re-educated away from unrealistic expectations of retirement. Social reform is predicated upon the promotion of independence among citizens, reflected in the modernizing agenda for local authority social services departments, with social work forming a key plank in the governance of citizens, and particularly problematic families (Jordan 2000). Responsibilization is achieved through inducement, targeting and the active promotion of independence, epitomized by the Department of Health's *Modernising Social Services* (1998b) and its emphasis upon 'independence', 'dignity', 'strengthening family life' and tackling 'youth crime' (paras 1.8, 1.12). As Jordan (2000: 84) expresses it, 'generalised safety nets' are to be replaced by 'customised trampolines'.

Similarly, the needs of children and families have been replaced by the risks of harm and the requirement to protect children from significant harm. Eligibility for provision is no longer needs-led and preventative, it is entirely investigative, forensic and risk-based. The social engineering of families is located within the forensic functions of child protection work. Families that cannot parent and self-regulate will be assisted to do so, and children who are 'at risk' will receive state protection. This will be delivered through an assessment system framed by judicial processes and forensic investigations. This system not only holds families to account for harmful behaviours; it holds workers and managers to account for their decision-making. Central to such decisions are issues of blame, defensibility and rationing. The social work of the personal social services is no longer about collectivist provision to those sections of society deemed to be 'in need', it is a residual service for those both at risk and posing a risk.

Suggestions for further reading

Alaszewski, A., Harrison, L. and Manthorpe, G. (1998) *Risk, Health and Welfare.* Buckingham: Open University Press. This book explores the impact of risk on health and social care. The impact on policy and practice, and the issues raised for workers, are particularly well covered.

Jordan, B. with Jordan, C. (2000) *Social Work and the Third Way: Tough Love as Social Policy.* London: Sage. This book explores New Labour welfare policy in the arena of social work, particularly the application of 'tough love', responsibilization and the meaning of active citizenship for social work clients.

chapter

five

Mental health, mental disorder, risk and public protection

Introduction

Mental health provision is one arena in which needs, rights and risks have long competed. In the Middle Ages the mentally ill were risk managed through expulsion or incarceration and exclusion through the 'ship of fools' (Foucault 1965). The Enlightenment provided an early example of privatized mental health care through profit-oriented 'madhouses'. The Victorian period and the early twentieth century were dominated by the spectre of the asylum and the concept of containment (Foucault 1965), although the walls between asylum and local communities were often permeable (Bartlett and Wright 1999) and 'lunatics' could be just as much 'at risk' in the community as in the asylum (Melling 1999). The deinstitutionalization of the post-Second World War period was based upon a consensus that large institutions were dehumanizing and prone to abusive relationships with patients. The anti-psychiatry movement in particular recast the asylum itself as a place of risk, and most mental health patients were seen as presenting a low or tolerable risk to the community if released. The latter part of the twentieth century saw the development of community care for the mentally ill. Carpenter (2000) has presented this deinstitutionalization as in part a response to the fiscal crisis of post-1945 welfare provision and advances in neo-liberal techniques of social control – in particular, the dispersal of the asylums' power and social control functions to the individual in the community through the 'psy' disciplines of psychiatry and psychology. The state's overt control is displaced to the control of experts and professionals, and the self-regulation of the individual through adaptation to the preset norms of the normalizing disciplines (Rose 1985, 1986a). As Carpenter (2000: 605) expresses it, the widening of social control is achieved through 'a co-optative rather than a repressive process'. Fiscally, community care (or community neglect, as Scull has dubbed it), has become a cheap alternative for the management of 'labour market casualties' in post-Keynesian markets (Scull 1979, 1993). Pilgrim and Rogers (1999) have identified four key elements in the development of community care provision:

• fiscal crisis in post-1945 welfare provision, resulting in deinstitutionalization;
• the rise and dominance of drug and physical treatments;
• the influence of cost-effective considerations and concerns with evidence-based treatments;
• the rise and influence of user groups and civil liberty considerations in mental health policy and provision.

This has been paralleled by mental health legislation such as the 1983 Mental Health Act, which reduced the medical orientation of mental health services to incorporate increased emphasis upon individual rights, support services and social needs (Fennell 1999). Ryan (1996) has expressed the history of mental health risk management in six stages, with distinct risk management strategies and sites of management (see Table 5.1).

The Community Care Act 1990 was followed by a policy emphasis upon partnership and coordination of services epitomized by the 'Care Programme Approach' (CPA: Department of Health 1990a), and practice guidance for care management (Department of Health 1991e). Care management and its predecessor, case management, were seen as essential techniques for adequately meeting client need and coordinating disparate resources into 'care packages' (Ryan *et al.* 1999). Case management was short-lived and focused upon the assessment and delivery of care in the community by health

Table 5.1   The history of risk management

Period	Risk management strategy	Risk management site
Middle Ages	Expulsion	Banishment and ships of fools
Enlightenment	Confinement	Private jails and madhouses
Victorian era	Incarceration	Asylums
Early twentieth century	Treatment	Psychiatric hospitals
Mid-twentieth century	Decarceration	Community
Late twentieth century	Integration	Community

Source: Ryan (1996: 101). Reproduced with the kind permission of Jessica Kingsley Publishers.

care professionals within a needs-led model (Onyett 1992). Care management, with its emphasis upon developing and managing care packages, superseded the needs-led approach with service-led control of provision under the umbrella of the CPA. The 1990s saw the tensions between risks, needs and rights in mental health provision sharpen. Risk became central to decisions made by approved social workers to detain mentally ill persons compulsorily under the Mental Health Act 1983. Risk reduction also became central to assessment and provision under the CPA (Davis 1996). However, as Davis (1996: 109–10) puts it,

> Risk is . . . emerging as a key but contested concern in the mental health field. It is being discussed in a climate in which political, professional, organisational and service users' interests and territories are being actively re-negotiated. It is thus important in considering risk work to take continuous account of the political, professional and resource interests that are influencing its development and direction.

Davis identifies two such developments: risk reduction and risk taking.

Risk reduction

The risk reduction approach has been fuelled by a series of high-profile mental health inquiries, such as Georgina Robinson (Blom-Cooper *et al.* 1995) and Christopher Clunis (Ritchie *et al.* 1994), which exposed flaws in the community care system to meet the care needs of the individuals concerned and to protect the public from risk. The CPA was introduced in 1991 to coordinate both assessment and interventions across a wide range of agencies and professionals, and risk, to both self and others, is seen as integral (Department of Health 1994a). This was supported by the Blom-Cooper inquiry, which stressed the 'ongoing assessment of risk and risk-management, assuming that risk will change over time and can be managed effectively' (Blom-Cooper *et al.* 1995: 176). CPA also used risk to prioritize cases, using a tiered approach comprising 'minimal', 'low support needs which are likely to remain stable' and 'complex' assessments for those whose needs are 'less likely to remain stable' (Davis 1996). Resource-intensive multidisciplinary assessments are reserved for those individuals 'suffering from severe social dysfunction, whose needs are likely to be highly volatile, or who represent a significant risk' (Department of Health 1994b). This has focused attention (and services) upon a small residual group of 'high-risk' individuals who are deemed to present a danger to the public. Provision has been skewed towards the identification, assessment, registration and surveillance of this group, and as 'a consequence it fails to engage adequately with the issues of risk as they affect the majority of service users' (Davis 1996: 113).

Risk taking

Risk taking has its roots in user empowerment, service user involvement and anti-oppressive mental health practice, and is seen as a necessary part of life and a right of mental health users (Braye and Preston-Shoot 1995). Normalization rather than risk reduction is a key feature of this approach, and risk is seen as integral to autonomy, quality of life and citizenship (Ramon 1991, Brown and Smith 1992). This approach is underpinned by radical values of empowerment and structural change:

> On the one hand are values located in a long tradition of social care. These urge practitioners to 'treat people better' in the context of allotted roles and place in the social structure. On the other hand are values calling for radical change to, and renegotiation of, existing roles and social structures, to create a fairer society. Thus the traditional agenda is to bring about the adjustment of service users to existing conditions in society, a focus on personal problems. The radical agenda emphasises the structural context in which problems are produced and reproduced.
> (Braye and Preston-Shoot 1995: 35–6)

Risk taking is often advocated by user groups, and is used to challenge the oppressive or restraining practices of professionals. It can thereby form an important limit to risk reduction as the bases of decisions to limit rights or choices have to be explicit and competing risks and rights have to be balanced (MIND 1986; Carson 1988, 1990, 1994, 1996). It has also been seen as essential to the reduction of stigma, dependency and over-protectiveness, a common feature in the lives of the mentally ill (Barham and Hayward 1991). However, while community care and risk taking have emphasized client needs and rights, in reality mental health risks have been increasingly negatively defined and community care has become focused on how to increase compliance with community treatments and surveillance (Ryan 1996). Mental health is now dominated by concerns with low-frequency/high-impact risks of homicide and suicide, with the high-frequency/low-impact risks faced by users in their daily lives largely neglected (Ryan 2000).

Summary

Deinstitutionalization and the shift to community care have sharpened attention to risk, particularly in assessment and resource provision. However, risk is a 'contested' area in which risk reduction and risk taking can be at odds, and the user's right to take risks is dominated by professional views of risk reduction. Community care has become preoccupied with risk avoidance and risk management, resulting in a largely negative view of user risks and a deprioritizing of user rights.

Mental health risks in the risk society

Frank Furedi (1997: 4) has argued that the 'evaluation of everything from the perspective of safety is a defining characteristic of contemporary society'. This 'worship of safety' is a key characteristic of life in the risk society, focusing attention on 'hazards' and 'threat' and prudent responses to them. As Furedi (1997: 4–5) puts it, 'By turning risk into an autonomous, omnipresent force in this way, we transform every human experience into a safety situation.' Human activity is characterized by risk aversion, and risk regulation is characterized by the 'precautionary principle'. Paradoxically this can lead us to over-perceive risks and to be fearful even in conditions of comparative safety. Media inflation of risks (Kitzinger 1999) and a lack of 'lay' trust in expert systems to regulate risks have exacerbated this. Mental health risks are no exception. The Mental Health Advisory Committee to the National Association for the Care and Resettlement of Offenders (NACRO) noted that while community care had 'placed the public at a slightly greater risk' this was not because the risks presented by mentally ill people were unacceptably high, but was due to failures in the system and the resource-led rather than needs-led nature of provision (NACRO 1998: 48). Mental health risk management failures have also heightened public and policy-makers' views that professional work with this group requires increased regulation and accountability (Sheppard 1996). Professional decision-making also takes place in a climate of blame, and exhortations to 'defensible decisions' abound (Carson 1996). Blame serves to strengthen accountability, but also subtly to control information flow and usage, and to reinforce loyalty and solidarity with particular viewpoints on risk: 'News that is going to be accepted as true information has to be wearing a badge of loyalty to the particular political regime which the person supports; the rest is suspect, deliberately censored or unconsciously ignored' (Douglas 1992: 19). In mental health practice this can result in the legitimization of professional views on risk at the expense of user or carer views. Competing views of risk result, not least between 'lay' public and experts. The subjectivity of risk assessment is now largely accepted (Royal Society Study Group 1992), but the responsibility of professionals to make the 'right decision' is emphasized by the power of hindsight bias. While the position on practitioner liability is less clear in the UK, cases such as W v. *Edgell* have clearly indicated that professionals should err on the side of public protection (Prins 1999). Professionals are also charged with deciding acceptable risk, a difficult task in an era of competing perspectives and values on risk.

Mental health has also long been a site of contested concepts, diagnoses, taxonomies and interventions, as evidenced by contemporary histories of insanity and psychiatry (Shorter 1997; Melling and Forsythe 1999) and historical sociological analyses of madness and its management (Scull 1979). As Table 5.1 indicates, definitions of, and responses to, mental disorder are also products of their time. Based upon detailed historical research, Scull has argued that the development of the Victorian asylum owes much to the weakening of community ties and traditional management techniques of mental disorder by the modernization of economic life and labour relations. The 'social casualties' of the emerging modern market environment were dealt with through institutionalization, and the purpose of such asylums was to

> model social behaviour around the norms of rational bourgeois expectations. Damaged human capital was repaired and worthless labour was warehoused in the corridors and buildings which quickly became museums filled with lifeless artefacts of humanity.
>
> (Melling 1999: 3)

The 'history of madness' has been characterized as a complex interaction between labour regulation, penal regulation and the development of medical practices to discipline the population (Foucault 1965), key intersections in the modernization process (Melling 1999).[1] While such historical constructions are themselves often contested, what is clear is that mental health has a long association with the process of modernization and the problem of order. As Harris (1999: 10) puts it, 'Looking at how we comprehend the seemingly irrational few tells us how we comprehend, without even thinking about them, the taken-for-granted seemingly rational many.' Mental disorder is therefore always defined with reference to an often unspoken and implicit norm. Defining mental health, especially as 'risky', is also central to the identification and solidarity of the included, as well as the exclusion of the 'other' (Douglas 1992). While the asylums have closed, the mentally ill are still with us and have become a site of control and public protection (Bartlett 1997).

Mental health and social order

Bartlett has argued that the legacy of the asylum runs deep, and is still the defining metaphor of mental health care today.

As Porter (1987: 35) has expressed it, we have 'a deep disposition to see madness as essentially Other'. This is not merely a matter of management or the administration of key services, it defines 'the terms on which people with mental illness are to be accepted in social life' (Bartlett 1997: xiii). The role of mental health provision and its attendant discipline psychiatry in defining the excluded and alienated other against a rational norm has been well argued:

> Society has progressively defined itself as rational and normal, and by doing so has sanctioned the stigmatizing and exclusion of 'outsiders'

and 'aliens'. And the particular device of the walled and locked asylum – which after all ended up housing far larger populations than did prisons – backed by the medical speciality of institutional psychiatry . . . under-scored the differentness, the uniqueness, of those thus 'alienated' and 'excluded'.

(Porter 1987: 25)

Thus processes of deinstitutionalization can themselves stigmatize and dehumanize, and mentally ill persons in the community can find themselves both alienated and socially isolated.

From mental patient to mental health case

The deinstitutionalization movement gathered pace by the 1960s, and institutional psychiatry was increasingly replaced by the notion of the 'therapeutic community', in which hospitals would provide brief respite and short-term treatment before reintegrating the patient into the community. Significantly, this reintegration was not based upon any acceptance of difference or counteraction of exclusion, but was aimed at abolishing difference through treatments that would normalize (Bartlett 1997). Patients would accommodate to their environments through the use of drug treatment and medication. For Bartlett, this rendered the community or environment a neutral venue, not a site of dispute, conflict, risk or threat to patients, merely a place to which they could be returned. Social sites would not require management, but individual patients would, and drug regimes, particularly administered through outpatients clinics, fitted the bill. While psychiatry managed to throw off its institutional custodial function, this function was subtly relocated to the community. The long-term and often immutable label 'mental patient' was replaced with the more provisional label 'mentally ill person' (Bartlett 1997), and in the case management language of the Community Care Programme the person became a 'mental health case'.

Community care provision for the mentally ill has been subject to the same limits of resource constraint and selectivism as other areas of the personal social services (see Chapter 4). Paradoxically, this has resulted in the invisibility of the majority of mentally ill persons and increased attention to the identification and regulation of a few high-risk cases. This trend is compounded by the tiered priorities for intervention and provision under the CPA, in which instability, significant risk and severe social dysfunction are essential criteria for intensive services. The Mental Health Foundation, in a report on community care provision for severe mental illness, has estimated that there are some 300,000 people with severe mental illness in England and Wales, but the report acknowledges that defining the term 'severe mental illness' is problematic, and conditions change (Mental Health Foundation 1994). This difficulty is exacerbated by mental health legislation that has traditionally defined mental illness and provided various taxonomies of illness to assist with compulsory admissions and detentions. Such legal definitions of mental illness have a limited role in classifying mental illness when its management is displaced to the community.

The invisibility of mentally ill persons not only prevents appropriate access to services, it also compounds their vulnerability. The vulnerabilities and risks of the asylum are merely displaced to the community, with ex-patients suffering abuse, poverty and social isolation (Bartlett 1997). The inadequacy of community care services to respond to this group was highlighted in various reports, with the National Schizophrenia Fellowship (1989) using the metaphor of 'Slipping through the net' to describe the problem. Such 'nets of care' come under scrutiny when they are deemed to have failed, and the invisibility of the majority is brought into sharp contrast with the minority who become the subject of inquiries. While the 1975 White Paper *Better Services for the Mentally Ill* (DHSS 1975) had accepted that the majority of mentally ill people were not especially dangerous and could therefore be appropriately managed in the community, the inquiries of the 1990s in particular focused attention on the few for whom, with hindsight, community care was deemed inappropriate. The Butler Committee in 1975 had attempted to define and introduce a two-tier system of mental health care, with the high-risk minority being selected out for secure hospital accommodation (Home Office and DHSS 1975). This, and the Glancy report (DHSS 1974), established the system of special hospitals and regional secure units for the 'dangerously' mentally ill. However, as the more recent NACRO review makes clear, the underlying assumption that it would be possible to identify and separate high- from low-risk patients was misplaced, and reliable risk assessment tools have been illusive (NACRO 1998; Prins 1999).

Mental health inquiries and the failure of community care

A major impetus in the move to community care was to ensure greater and more relevant provision for the mentally ill from health and social services, epitomized by the document *Better Services for the Mentally Ill*. Central to government policy on mental health was the introduction of the CPA in 1990 (Department of Health 1990a, b). The CPA emphasized assessment, a care plan, an allocated key worker for each case and regular review of progress. The CPA represented an acknowledgement that the principles of community care following hospital closures required tighter structures and systems for their delivery. However, resources remained a key issue in the adequate delivery of the CPA (Davis 1996; Ryan 1996). Disquiet about the adequate management of mentally ill persons in the community was fuelled by what Grounds (1996) refers to as a new generation of inquiry reports from the late 1980s onwards, in which the focus of attention was homicides perpetrated by mentally ill persons. These reports attracted greater media attention and public disquiet than their predecessors, which had focused on the abuse of patients in psychiatric institutions. The most notable of these were Christopher Clunis (Ritchie *et al.* 1994), Andrew Robinson (Blom-Cooper 1996) and the two overviews of inquiries prepared by Sheppard (1997, 1998). The inquiries highlighted specific procedural and systems failures in the care of dangerous and violent mentally ill persons in the community.

The reports highlighted the following:

- inadequate coordination and poor communication between professionals and agencies;
- lack of appropriate resources, including secure beds as well as community provision;
- the need for special supervision arrangements;
- inadequate information sharing and recording;
- inadequate and unreliable assessment of risk and violent behaviour;
- lack of cooperation between agencies;
- patients' rights required greater attention, in particular the right to have their needs met, and to express their needs, wishes and choices;
- legislation required attention, in particular for supervision on discharge from hospital and for compulsory treatment and supervision in the community (adapted from NACRO 1998: 24; Sheppard 1997, 1998).

The cumulative impact of the inquiry recommendations and their attendant publicity subtly moved the mental health agenda from care to management, and from treatment and rehabilitation to control and surveillance. Risk and protection began to dominate the mental health policy agenda (Grounds 1996). This is evidenced by:

- specific policy development and practice guidance on mental health management of high-risk cases in the community and the development of compulsory community care;
- the increased attention to mentally disordered offenders;
- the development of preventative detention for high-risk cases.

Summary

Risk avoidance and the 'worship of safety' are key features of mental health policy. The 'history of madness' has been characterized as a history of social regulation and normalization of the 'Other', in which segregation, surveillance and control of the mentally ill are central. The metaphoric segregation of the asylum is still pervasive in the constitution of community care, with social control functions transferred from asylum to community. Deinstitutionalization is not characterized by reintegration, but by the invisibility of 'low-risk cases' on the one hand and extensive management of more risky individuals on the other, resulting in a two-tier system of mental health provision. Individualization through individual targeting shifts attention from structural issues and social site management to regulating the behaviours of individuals and compensating for any lack of prudentialism or risk management. Responsibility for risk is firmly individual, either of the worker or patient-worker for failing to manage it effectively, or of patients for failing to comply with risk management strategies. The failure of such strategies inevitably attracts public and media attention, and community care has been subject to regular and notorious public inquiries on its shortcomings.

Mental health management and the development of community care

The inquiry into the care and after-care of Sharon Campbell (Spokes *et al.* 1988) and the case of Benjamin Silcock, who injured himself by climbing into the lion's den at London Zoo, prompted the then Secretary of State for Health, Virginia Bottomley, to announce a 'ten point plan' to strengthen community care for the severe mentally ill (Department of Health 1993). The main objective of the plan was to close loopholes in current arrangements and to prevent people from 'slipping through the net'. By 1994 supervision registers for high-risk or potentially high-risk mentally ill persons and guidance on the discharge of patients from hospital were introduced (Department of Health 1994a). These measures were designed to assist in identification of those most risky, and to target appropriate resources and strengthen care plans. This was seen as particularly pertinent for hospital discharge, in which levels of risk were seen as crucial, and appropriate supervision and support were seen as absolute requirements post-release. The issue of formalized and expert risk assessments was addressed in official documents for the first time, and communication of confidential information to other agencies without the patient's consent was seen as justified if protection of the public required it. The Mental Health (Patients in the Community) Act 1995 introduced supervision discharge for patients where a substantial risk to either the patients' safety or other persons could be demonstrated, thus ensuring access to after-care services but also introducing compulsory supervision and monitoring on the grounds of risk (section 117). This Act represents a watershed in mental health care policy and legislation, as it shifts attention from community care to the majority and from issues of community reintegration to the identification and effective management of potential dangerousness. As Fennell (1999: 107) puts it, 'From 1993 onwards the . . . government introduced measures designed to require patients to accept medicine in the community.' The Act could also require discharged patients to live at a specified address, to attend for medical treatment, education or training and to permit mental health professionals (such as community psychiatric nurses) to enter their home. Failure to comply with these conditions could result in a compulsory admission.

Work across agencies and inter-agency partnerships were also advocated as responses to inquiry shortcomings. The Clunis Report in particular had highlighted the failure of inter-agency communication and cooperation, and the Mitchell Report (Blom-Cooper 1996) advocated adoption of child protection multi-agency systems. The Department of Health report *Building Bridges* (1995) not only reviewed existing systems but recommended inter-agency working as a key mechanism in the effective delivery of the CPA. This began a long-term policy initiative to develop and extend the 'care nets' and to ensure that there was no subsequent slippage. However, by the time New Labour entered office in 1997 the 1995 Act was failing to bite. While it had been estimated that around 3000 patients would benefit from community supervision (Royal College of Psychiatrists 1993), Fennell concludes that the power has been little used. By 1998 the Secretary of State for Health, Frank Dobson, had declared that community care had failed and that he wanted a 'third way' in mental health provision, to include a 'root and branch' review of legislation 'to reflect the opportunities and limits of modern therapies and drugs' (Fennell 1999: 104; see also Department of Health 1998c). Minister Paul Boateng articulated the government's preoccupation with risk and safety:

with our safety plus approach, the law must make it clear that non-compliance with agreed treatment programmes is not an option. We are determined to develop comprehensive mental health services which are safe, sound and supportive. They must protect the public and provide safe and effective care for mentally ill people. New legislation is needed to support our new policies, for example to provide extra powers to treat patients in a range of clinical settings including, where necessary, in the community, and to ensure the proper balance between the interests of the public and the rights of the individual. Carers too should have rights, as well as responsibilities. Too often they have been left to pick up the pieces, but were never given any rights at the moment of a crisis affecting those for whom they have been responsible.
(From Fennell 1999: 110)

This is in sharp contrast to the vision of civic participation and reintegration advocated for mental health services by Tomlinson (1991) and Bartlett (1997). In addition to the Mental Health Act 1995, mental health provision is now underpinned by a range of legislation and policy documents, including the Crime and Disorder Act 1998, *Building Bridges* (Department of Health 1995), *The Spectrum of Care* (Department of Health 1996) and guidance for the discharge and supervision of patients (Department of Health

1994a). As O'Rourke and Hammond (2000: 2) put it, 'The need for a comprehensive risk management strategy for mental health has never been greater.' Two key developments in the delivery of compulsory community risk management under the community care umbrella can be discerned:

- assertive outreach (Ryan 1999; Ryan *et al.* 1999);
- RAMAS, or 'risk assessment, management and audit systems' (O'Rourke and Hammond 2000).

Assertive outreach

Assertive outreach was proposed by Frank Dobson in his 'root and branch' review of mental health services in 1998 to provide mental health teams who could engage with and monitor 'at-risk' service users (Department of Health 1999c; Ryan *et al.* 1999: 97–8). In essence it is an intensive case management system designed to match intensity of resources to client need and risk, and to coordinate services across a range of agencies. The model stresses continuity of care and high-quality relationships between key worker and user. Ryan *et al.* found that case management teams were 'highly successful in the co-ordination aspects of their work' but that users tended to be linked to available resources rather than have their expressed needs genuinely met – the perennial problem of community care. They concluded that 'case management is only as effective as the supporting services which are available' (Ryan *et al.* 1999: 113). This resulted in variable results and, given the greater costs involved in assertive outreach, benefits were marginal in some areas. They advocated that mental health case management should be costed on the Challis and Davies (1986) model from care of the elderly; that is, the weekly cost of case provision should not exceed two-thirds of residential care. In this way a 'value for money ethos' can be inculcated into case managers. While they conclude that both the effectiveness and cost-efficiency of assertive outreach are still unproven, they state that within the context of current government policy:

> case management (or assertive outreach as the new policy review will describe it) continues to be not so much the 'treatment of choice' as *the only viable mechanism* for ensuring that a highly vulnerable 'at risk' client group can be engaged in services and responded to in a needs-led manner. In other words, case management prevents users from 'falling through the net', and ensures that they receive an appropriate, individually tailored network of services. The furore that has attended the tragedies surrounding Christopher Clunis (Ritchie *et al.* 1994) and many others is surely sufficient to remind us of the vital importance of these achievements.
>
> (Ryan *et al.* 1999: 121)

Intensive CPA programmes for high-risk offenders based upon assertive outreach were set to replace Supervision Registers by April 2001 (NHS Executive 1999).

RAMAS: risk assessment, management and audit systems

RAMAS was also developed in response to the Clunis public inquiry and the perceived failure of community care (O'Rourke and Hammond 2000). The system attempts to incorporate lessons from public inquiries, most notably to ensure that 'people who pose a risk to themselves or others do not "fall through the net" of treatment and care' and to provide 'public safety' through inter-agency collaboration. The model also emphasizes workload management, and following the Department of Health's (1998c) modernizing agenda for mental health services, clinical governance, audit and evidence-based practice are also highlighted. Clinical governance in particular is seen as a quality assurance system to avoid risks, and to learn rapidly from 'adverse events'. The model provides a 'common language to provide clear and shared goals for public safety', and is unequivocal about its main objective of identifying and reducing risk. The purpose of risk management is defined as 'risk minimisation and the provision of safe, sound, supportive services'. O'Rourke and Hammond take the Department of Health's own definition of 'safe, sound and supportive services' as their starting point:

- *Safe:* to protect the public and provide effective care for those with mental illness when they need it.
- *Sound:* to ensure that patients and service users have access to the full range of services that they need.
- *Supportive:* working with patients and service users, their families and carers to build healthier communities (from O'Rourke and Hammond 2000: 10, see Department of Health 1998c).

The emphasis upon public safety, risk management and audit has tended to result in increasingly forensic approaches to risk (Douglas 1992; Kemshall *et al.* 1997) and concerns to predict and avert potentially dangerous events and minimize risk at all costs. This trend is illustrated by responses to mentally disordered offenders and the extension of community care *as risk management* to the mental health population at large.

Mentally disordered offenders

This 'net-widening' of risk concerns to the mental health population at large and to those approaching discharge has been paralleled by increased attention to mentally disordered offenders. Pilgrim and Rogers (1999) have identified the preoccupation with risk and violence at the macro level, and the transformation of mental health policy into a risk management policy for 'dangerous' persons. Mental health, mental disorder and 'dangerousness' have become synonymous. The Reed Report represents an important stage in both approach and services to this group (Department of Health and Home Office 1992b). The report was initiated partly in response to the growing split between general and forensic mental health services and the recognition that mentally disordered persons in prisons were suffering from a lack of appropriate treatment. The review recognized that the label 'mentally disordered offender' covers a range of offenders in the criminal justice system, few of whom represent a significant risk of danger to others. The report took the view that the majority of such offenders could and should be dealt with in the community and that access to and coordination of community services should be improved: 'In line with current policy, mentally disordered offenders should, wherever possible, receive care and treatment from health or social services rather than in the criminal justice system' (Department of Health and Home Office 1992b: para. 11.1).

The Reed Report also recommended early identification and assessment of mentally disordered offenders in the criminal justice system, and where possible diversion from police and prison custody to the care of health or social services (p. 14). However, as Cavadino (1999) points out, this resulted in an over-emphasis upon court diversion schemes and assessment, with rather less attention on long-term services in the community for those diverted. This resulted in something of a 'revolving door' between community, police station and court. In volume two of their report the Reed committee also noted that 'courts remand the mentally disordered in custody essentially for psychiatric and social reasons rather than for reasons of public safety or seriousness of offence'. In essence the committee wished to prevent mentally disordered offenders entering the prison system via the remand route. This supported Home Office guidance (Home Office Circular 66/90), which stated that 'a mentally disordered offender should never be remanded to prison simply to receive medical treatment or assessment'. Subsequent policy guidance supported the view that 'mentally disordered people who require treatment and support because of their health care needs should be cared for or treated . . . as far as possible, in the community rather than in institutional settings' (Home Office and Department of Health 1995: 12). However, while there have been some notable successes in pre-court and court based assessment and diversion, Cavadino (1999: 67) concludes from a Home Office commissioned NACRO study that 'some of the funding arrangements are fragile, for example, dependent on a single local agency (mostly health trusts or district authorities) where there is no long-term commitment'.

However, diversion has yet to be fully integrated into mainstream services. The early 1990s impetus towards diversion of the low-risk many has largely been over-shadowed by attention to the high-risk few (Davis 1996; Ryan

1996; Foster 1998). This has been fuelled by the volume of inquiries in the 1990s, and the growing culture of litigation and blame (Carson 1996). Ryan has argued that this has resulted in providers of mental health services becoming risk-averse organizations and subsequently controlling the assessments and interventions of front-line practitioners to avoid error and litigation. Such caution necessarily militates against the rehabilitation and empowerment values held by staff. Risk-averse cultures can inhibit the reintegrative functions of social care. This has been particularly acute in mental health work with offenders. While homicides by psychiatric patients and mentally disordered offenders are rare (Boyd 1996), the inquiries in the 1990s focused attention on the appropriate community regulation of such people, and the inquiry into Jason Mitchell (Blom-Cooper 1996) focused attention on inter-agency communication and appropriate responses to mentally disordered offenders. The report recommended that the Crown Prosecution Service should prepare full details of the account, disseminate full information to the Home Office and clinicians responsible for the offender/patient and, where public safety is an issue, obtain an independent forensic psychiatric assessment of risk (NACRO 1998).

This emphasis upon risk prevention and the reduction of harm to the public by mentally disordered offenders was paralleled by extensive changes in the parole system. The Criminal Justice Act 1991 introduced new arrangements for parole in England and Wales, in which the risk of reoffending, especially of violent offending, was made the key determining factor in deciding release. Public protection and the prevention of significant harm became central to parole decision-making (Home Office 1992). This also encompassed mentally disordered offenders, often regarded by lay persons as particularly risky, and the parole board has a responsibility to consider medical and psychiatric factors as significant dynamic risk factors (Ditchfield 1997). This responsibility was reinforced by the Parole Board Annual Report (1994: 4) which stated:

> We have been increasingly troubled at the release of potentially violent prisoners with psychiatric problems . . . those prisoners sentenced to four years and over after 1 October 1992 have gone out into the community with probation support; and they have also benefited from psychiatric oversight, hostel accommodation and offence-related licence. Further, victims have been protected by 'no contact' conditions which forbid the prisoner to contact named people or return to named locations during the licence period . . . However, we have remained concerned not only about the high risk of offending posed by these prisoners, but about our own capacity to predict this risk and to identify the best way of accommodating these special needs.

This led to an increased concern with risk assessment tools and methods for use in the prediction of violent and sexual reoffending (Kemshall 1998).

While some tools have been pioneered (for example, the parole reconvictor: Copas *et al.* 1996), accurate prediction of 'dangerous offenders' and particularly dangerous mentally disordered offenders has remained a perennial problem (Prins 1999). Procedurally parole boards have also attempted to improve their practice through training, guidance from the Royal College of Psychiatrists to their members providing psychiatric reports on prisoners and the use of expert psychiatric personnel on boards in relevant cases. Boards also have a key role in adding conditions to licences; for example, of treatment, residence, supervision and negative requirements such as 'no contact'. Such supervision is carried out by the probation service, and high-risk offenders can be referred to and discussed at multi-agency risk management panels, which usually comprise police, probation, social services and health personnel (Maguire *et al.* 2000). Such panels are a relatively recent initiative for sexual and other potentially high-risk offenders, and it is too early to determine the volume of mentally disordered offenders coming to panels or the efficacy of such panels in this area of work.

The rise of preventive measures for mentally disordered persons

The report into the Andrew Robinson case (Blom-Cooper *et al.* 1995) extended the notion of compulsory community care beyond those who had been the subject of hospital treatment under the 1983 Mental Health Act. The report proposed 'secure care' and treatment in a designated place, which could include the patient's home. While the Royal College of Psychiatrists has largely resisted the growing trend to compulsory community interventions, compulsion has continued as a key trend in mental health policy (Fennell 1999). By the end of the 1990s, prevention had also joined the mental health policy agenda. This move was again influenced by risk, particularly the risk presented by a small group of people suffering from severe personality disorder and deemed to present a significant risk of harm to the public. The impetus again came from a single case in which a man suffering from severe personality disorder but deemed untreatable by psychiatric services killed a mother and severely injured her child. The case attracted extensive media coverage, not least due to the apparent failure of the mental health net to manage the perpetrator effectively, and to the problem of effectively treating severe personality disorder. In particular, the 'untreatable' clause of the Mental Health Act 1983 in effect makes compulsory admission and detention for those in the 'untreatable' category impossible.

In February 1999 the Home Secretary announced new proposals for the management of mentally disordered persons with severe personality disorder. In *Managing Dangerous People with Severe Personality Disorder* the Home Office identified a small group of people with severe personality disorder, calculated at approximately 2000 people in England and Wales (Home Office and Department of Health 1999). The proposals aimed to prevent the discharge of such people from prison or hospital while they still posed a significant risk of harm to the public. In addition, the proposals aimed to introduce preventative detention for those suffering a severe personality disorder and who pose a significant risk to public safety but who are deemed untreatable under the Mental Health Act 1983, thus closing a loophole. The Home Office document categorizes the 'overwhelming majority' of such persons as 'people who have committed serious offences such as murder, manslaughter, arson, serious sex offences, or grievous bodily harm' (p. 9). The estimated proportion of people who fit this criterion is 'between 300 and 600 men', with the figures for juveniles and women estimated as 'very low' (p. 9). The proposals are particularly concerned with:

- the creation of new legislative powers for the extended detention and supervision of dangerous severe personality disordered individuals;
- identification and risk assessment based upon agreed national protocols and assessment tools;
- long-term case management and the development of best practice management strategies to reduce risk to the public.

In effect, these proposals represent the extension of detention powers based upon risk, in which risk and not health would form both the basis of compulsory treatment and determine readiness for release. The proposals would allow 'dangerous severe personality disordered' persons to be detained indefinitely (although subject to review) even if they remain untreatable, and even if they have not committed a violent (or any other) offence. It is worth noting that the label 'dangerous severe personality disorder' is a political term derived from government policy outlined in the Home Office consultation document (1999), and is not readily accepted as a medical term amenable to accurate diagnosis (Royal College of Psychiatrists 1999). The term has come into policy use even though there is no clinically accepted definition of it. The use of the term and the proposals are seen as a challenge both to clinicians and to the civil liberties of mentally ill persons (Royal College of Psychiatrists 1999). MIND, for example, in its evidence to the House of Commons Home Affairs Committee on the proposals, highlighted the lack of clinical agreement and evidence for the definition, and described the link to violence as circular:

> A person is labelled as having APD because they engage in violent behaviour and the reason they engage in violent behaviour is because they have APD. There seems to be a risk that the definition will be stretched to include whoever the Government or public opinion thinks at any particular point in time ought to be preventively detained.
>
> (MIND 1999: 6)

In addition, the MIND evidence presented current disquiet over the accuracy of risk assessment, stating that it was not an exact science, and that the number of likely false positives leading to preventative detention were unacceptably high. This unease at the potential number of false positives is shared by the Royal College of Psychiatrists, which estimates that it may be necessary to detain 50 people to prevent between five and ten committing a serious violent crime (Royal College of Psychiatrists 1999). The difficulties of accurate risk prediction are also noted by the Department of Health (1995), which describes risk assessment as an 'inexact science', and by the National Confidential Inquiry into Suicides and Homicides by People with Mental Illness (Department of Health 1999d), which noted the very low percentage of people labelled as high risk who went on to commit homicide. As Bingley (1997: 28) puts it, 'how many false positives is society prepared to accept in pursuit of a social goal?' The evidence from MIND suggests that the answer may be quite a lot unless government proposals are curtailed. Preoccupation with identifying a high-risk minority is fuelling public perceptions of mental disorder as both violent and risky, and the development and implementation of containment procedures for this group are leading attention and resources away from the majority of users who are at risk. The report of the Royal College of Psychiatrists (1999) also points out that psychiatry is not in a position to accept the mantle of identifying and controlling dangerous mentally ill people that current 'Third Way' policy dictates. The acceptance of such a responsibility 'would require a shift in emphasis from delivery of care in the community to surveillance and social control' (p. 47). One suspects that the shift is already well under way.

Summary

Mental health inquiries focused attention on the lack of compliance with mental health services. This resulted in legislative and policy change to introduce compulsory treatment in the community and compulsory post-release supervision for certain categories of discharged patients. Two key developments exemplify the preoccupation with risk: assertive outreach and the RAMAS assessment and case management system. Both developments are informed by the Department of Health's emphasis upon safe, sound and supportive services to mental health users. The emphasis upon compulsion and public safety is also evidenced in legislation and policy responses to mentally disordered offenders, which has culminated in proposed preventative measures for dangerous people with severe personality disorders. This has shifted the main purpose of mental health services and its attendant profession, psychiatry, from the treatment of mental disorder and care in the community to surveillance and social control.

Conclusions

The asylum and its predecessor the 'ship of fools' have been replaced by community care. However, deinstitutionalization has not been accompanied by a lessening of mental health risks. On the contrary, risk preoccupations have grown. While the old asylum may have disappeared, secure containment of the 'dangerous' mentally ill has increased. While the number of restricted patients convicted of murder or other homicide has remained relatively constant, the use of restriction orders for dangerously mentally ill people under the Mental Health Act 1983 has risen substantially over the past ten years (NACRO 1998: 10–13). Community care is increasingly characterized by risk, either the prevention of risk taking by mentally ill persons or the treatment and containment of risky behaviours deemed likely to compromise public safety. The care of the mentally ill outside of the asylum is dominated by compulsory treatment and containment. Significant legislative and policy changes have shifted the emphasis from rights to risks. As P. Ryan (1999: 4) expresses it:

> It seems clear from the White Paper (Department of Health 1998) that the primary task and role of mental health services will be that of protecting the public . . . The government clearly sees assertive outreach as a means of establishing service contact with, and tracking and monitoring high-risk and potentially violent clients.

The new mental health policy, as set out by the Department of Health (1998c), attempts to forge a 'Third Way' between care and control by emphasizing 'assertive outreach' for those who are resistant to services and for whom compulsory community care would enhance public safety. A balance between 'supportive services' and user entitlement on the one hand, and public safety and client control on the other, is advocated – an invidious position for those delivering mental health services. Newnes and Holmes (1999: 276) describe this as 'coercive psychiatry' predicated upon risk avoidance and risk management. They contend that:

> The terror of this destroys innovative practice and always leads to back-covering caution; to recommend someone does not take or stops taking medication . . . becomes frightening to a professional who fears they will be made responsible if the person later harms themselves or another person. Most of our resources are now being spent assessing, categorising and monitoring rather than helping people.

The link between social regulation, compulsory treatment and mental health is well established (Foucault 1978; Pilgrim and Rogers 1993) and segregative control through the use of asylums has a long history (Bartlett 1997). The deinstitutionalization of mental health services has seen the displacement of control to community mechanisms such as drug treatments, post-release supervision and assertive outreach. This has been paralleled by increased attention to assessment in order to distinguish the dangerously mentally ill from a low-risk invisible majority. A legal framework that emphasizes public protection and an individualistic response to mental health service users, in which problems are individually ascribed and the structural context of mental illness and its service delivery is obscured, supports such assessments (Rose 1986a, b; Pilgrim and Rogers 1993). Forensic psychiatry in particular has become dominated by issues of risk, in particular personality disorder and psychopathy (Pilgrim and Rogers 1999; Manning 2000). Psychiatry in this area is concerned not just with treatment, but with risk assessment and prediction, followed by compulsory detention or treatment on the grounds of public safety. The dominance of public safety as the key organizing principle of mental health services has been fuelled by media and public inquiries into community care failures (Muijen 1996). The result is a peculiar paranoia over risk:

Our society is in the grip of a movement towards everyone having either an official or moral duty to monitor people deemed to be deviant (e.g. paedophiles, illegal immigrants, benefits recipients, school truants, as well as people diagnosed as mentally ill).

(Newnes and Holmes 1999: 280)

Alaszewski (2000: 10) has described the 1990s as the 'risk decade' in health and welfare services, and this has certainly been the case in mental health. In this arena risk has become equated with danger, 'lots of danger' (Douglas 1992), and risk taking has been replaced by a culture of risk avoidance. However, as Alaszewski (2000: 11) argues, a broader approach to risk management would involve 'balancing the potential negatives and harmful consequences of decisions against the anticipated benefits, taking into account relative probabilities'. The present negative climate of risk assessment and management works against this, and policy is largely dominated by risk avoidance. In practice this results in a narrow, technicist approach to risk in which threat and danger are seen everywhere, and practitioners reduce the risk taking of users in order to minimize professional risks to themselves.

Despite the closure of the 'asylum', two-thirds of the mental health budget in the 1990s was still accounted for by hospital beds, although the number of beds has been drastically reduced (Audit Commission 1994b). As a result of this bed shortage and failure to transfer hospital funds to the community, admission thresholds are too high and community supports too low (Hanily 1999). This has placed mental health users 'at risk' (Ryan 1996), although such risks are largely invisible and inadequately dealt with (Davis 1996; Bartlett 1997). Ryan's contention in Table 5.1 that integration was the main risk management strategy of the late twentieth century is disputable. Current developments suggest that the twenty-first century is likely to see a combination of compulsory treatment and surveillance in the community for high-risk mentally ill persons, and isolation and invisibility as subtle mechanisms of community segregation for the low-risk (Bartlett and Sandland 2000).

Note

1 It is beyond the scope of this chapter to present a full overview of the 'history of madness'. For further illumination, and at times competing views, see Foucault (1965), Scull (1979) and Melling and Forsythe (1999).

Suggestions for further reading

Carpenter, M. (2000) 'It's a small world': mental health policy under welfare capitalism since 1945. *Sociology of Health and Illness*, 22(5), 602–20. This article charts the changes in mental provision post-1945 and links such changes to the restructuring of the welfare state in the late twentieth century.

MIND (1999) *Summary of Evidence to House of Commons Home Affairs Committee: Inquiry into the Government's Proposals for Managing Dangerous People with Severe Personality Disorder*. London: MIND. This briefing paper provides an excellent overview of the key issues in risk and dangerousness prediction for mentally disordered persons.

National Association for the Care and Resettlement of Offenders (NACRO) (1998) *Risk and Rights: Mentally Disturbed Offenders and Public Protection. A Report by NACRO's Mental Health Advisory Committee*. London: NACRO. This short monograph provides an overview of key policy documents, research and public inquiries.

chapter

six

The new risk-based welfare

Introduction

Rodger (2000: 3) has described the key principle of the 'new moral economy of welfare' as 'privatisation of responsibility'. This suggests a wholesale shift of state responsibility to the private sphere of individual, family and community, in which risk management is defined in largely individualist rather than collective terms. This book has sought to examine the extent of that shift, and how it is evidenced in certain key spheres of provision. The moral imperative of 'new welfare' emphasizes self-reliance and responsibilization, a key ingredient of which is the acknowledgement that the moral dependency of traditional welfare has failed (Saunders 1993; Rodger 2000). The Blair view of a welfare society based upon remoralized social citizenship is a key example, the 'something for something society' (Blair 1998b). This vision is encapsulated in the consultation document *New Ambition for Our Country: A New Contract for Welfare* (Department of Social Security 1998), which links 'rights to responsibilities' and argues for a 'new contract between citizen and state' (p. 1). Self-care, prudence and the work ethic are the cornerstone ingredients. As Rodger (2000: 5) expresses it, the duties of the individual are to:

- seek training or work where able to do so;
- take up the opportunity to be independent if able to do so;
- give support, financial or otherwise, to one's children and other family members;
- save for retirement where possible;
- refrain from defrauding the taxpayer.

Social policy in the twenty-first century can be characterized by concerns to remoralize social behaviour, redefine citizenship as proactive and responsibilized, and replace 'moral hazard' with the work ethic. Rodger argues that this represents a new 'activeness' in social policy, facilitating and encouraging citizens to do things, rather than a passive system based upon compensation for losses and ills. In essence, this represents a more active social policy engagement with risk: citizens are encouraged to be flexible and adaptive to the risks associated with rapid economic change, for example (Giddens 1998b), and individual rather than collective responsibility for risk management is promoted. The 'downsizing' of the welfare state and a recognition that welfarist social policy has failed to tackle social inequality have been key pressures in this shift. Rodger (2000: 7) labels this as a move from a welfare state to a welfare society:

> What is clear today is that either by chance or by design the state in the twenty first century is redrawing the boundaries of its responsibilities for the welfare of its citizens (see Millar and Warman 1996). We are moving away from the concept of the welfare state which provided, for most of its citizens, something which we called a *social wage*: a package of benefits which supplemented income from employment, pooled risks against unforeseen hardship through state-sponsored and managed insurance and provided a range of services underwritten by the state which were accessible to all . . . and moving towards a society in which family and community relationships are being required to take on a more explicit responsibility for sustaining the well-being of their members, based less on a commitment to a collective sense of social solidarity than on a sense of kindred obligation and charitable civic virtue.

In essence, the responsibility is now firmly with individuals for the purchase and management of their own 'welfare capital'.

Shifting welfare: consensus or difference?

The future of welfare in Britain is by no means clear cut. While the work of Giddens (1990, 1994, 1998b) and others (Murray 1990) has challenged the capacity of the traditional welfare state to alleviate the risks of individuals, how welfare, particularly state-centred welfare, should be restructured to meet the needs of the 'risk society' is contested. A number of key positions can be discerned, of which the following are reviewed:

- the Schumpterian workfare state;
- the 'dialogic democracy' of the Third Way;
- the responsibilization of the individual and advanced liberal goverance;
- postmodern welfare.

The Schumpeterian workfare state[1]

This position is best expressed in the work of Jessop (2000), who argues for the replacement of the traditional Keynesian welfare state by an innovative, open economy adaptive to post-Fordist market conditions in which social policy is subordinated to the needs of the labour market. Flexible production is the key ingredient of such nation states, characterized by changes in regulation and governance of both economic and social life. Market deregulation is coupled with an expansion of market forces into social life through privatization and the marketization of social relations and welfare 'products'. Social life is transformed by economic discourse, and the state apparatus is reconstituted economically and subjected to market forces. Education, for example, is subordinated to the needs of the labour market and a 'reorientation towards vocational training and "enterprise"' (Jessop 1994: 32). This also illustrates the 'supply side' concerns of the Schumpeterian workfare state (SWS) and the emphasis upon permanent innovation epitomized by notions of a highly skilled workforce committed to lifelong learning.

Jessop's position is not without its critics. Changes in social policy have not totally mirrored economic concerns or the shift to post-Fordism (Clarke and Newman 1997), and the routes to a SWS have also been in dispute. Jessop's later work identifies 'four ideal-type strategies' for moving to what he labels a Schumpeterian workfare post-national regime (Jessop 2000: 177). These are:

- Neo-liberalism, characterized as a 'market-led process of economic and social restructuring which uses privatisation, de-regulation, and marketisation of the state sector'. Flexible working and a flexible labour supply are emphasized, and the welfare state is transformed from a safety net against collective risks to a mechanism to supplement low wages (family credit, for example), and to discipline the marginalized workforce back into work (workfare). In effect, the state sponsors and facilitates an enterprise culture in which both capital and workers should embrace opportunities, be flexible and continually innovate. This approach is characterized by the final years of Thatcherism and John Major's conservatism. In part, New Labour policy is also informed by neo-liberalism.
- Neo-corporatism is characterized by a partnership to restructuring between private, public and third sectors. The key aim is a balance between competition and cooperation, but unlike in traditional Fordism, non-traditional partnerships are encouraged, and a range of policy communities and vested interest groups are incorporated. Power is held within these corporate arrangements rather than held solely at the centralized national level. To some extent the 'dialogic democracy' advocated by Giddens (1994: 112), which stresses the development of new political frameworks to enable the diversity of interest groups in late modern society to negotiate, is an example of this approach. However, as with the

neo-liberal approach, individual responsibility and flexible responses to opportunity (and to risk taking) are advocated.

- Neo-statism advocates state control but towards market-oriented ends. The state pursues activities which contribute to 'dynamic efficiency' and a 'productive economy' (Jessop 2000: 179). New technologies, technology transfer, continual innovation, infrastructures to support innovation and growth, and flexi-skilling of the workforce are all essential components. The state will also seek to safeguard technological and economic 'edge' from national competitors. This approach is illustrated by the policies of Japan and other states on the Pacific rim and in South East Asia.
- Neo-communitarianism emphasizes the contribution of the third sector or the 'social economy' to economic development and social cohesion. In this approach the key role of community and of community groups is emphasized, along with notions of empowerment, stakeholders and self-sufficiency. Social inclusion, particularly of marginalized spaces such as the inner city, and of marginalized communities, groups and individuals, is advocated, with added-value understood in social rather than economic terms, and with the generation and use of social capital seen as important as the generation and use of economic capital. Elements of Blairism stress communitarianism, although in terms of actual policy implementation this has remained largely rhetorical (Jessop 2000: 177–80).

Importantly, Jessop acknowledges some 'counter-trends' to these new welfare state forms. Most notable is the collapse of South East Asian economies as the epitomy of neo-statism, and of a form of SWS praised by British politicians in the Thatcher era. The so-called 'tiger economies' have not proven to have all the answers to post-Fordism and the problems of welfare. Rapid change in Eastern Europe has also provided a severe challenge to the transformation of welfare forms. As Jordan (1998) puts it, the pace of change and the impact of global markets is the central problem in such economies as they struggle with the transformation of their economies and societies from state communism to global capitalism. Jordan (1998: 229) has also pointed out that Eastern European countries such as Poland and Hungary have used social provision, especially social security, to ease the pains of this transition, and to ensure a degree of social cohesion and solidarity. Such states are more easily located within the traditional Keynesian model than in emerging post-Fordist models, and a Keynesian state form is viewed as a central mechanism in preserving social order at a time of great structural change, rather than as a barrier to achieving such change.

Within the European Union one can also discern differing degrees of post-Fordism, and differing strategies from the above in adapting to it. Britain, for example, is currently operating most clearly within a neo-liberal framework. While communitarianism and stakeholding indicate New Labour's acceptance of a social dimension (Heron and Dwyer 1999), New Labour social policy is still fundamentally concerned with regulating the behaviours of individual welfare recipients (Finer Jones 1997). This is most clearly espoused in *A New Contract for Welfare* (Department of Social Security 1998), in which the work ethic and social obligation are stressed. 'Duty' is at the heart of the new contract for welfare between the individual and the state (Heron and Dwyer 1999) and communitarian philosophy is constituted as moral order, collective community action to remoralize and revitalize society, and mutual social obligation. As Blair (1993: 3–4) put it, 'without responsibility there is no society'.

Caution has also been expressed about the ability of SWS welfare forms to avoid 'social dumping' and increased social exclusion (Jordan 1998; Jessop 2000). Social cohesion and solidarity have long been an aim of social policy (Lavalette and Pratt 1997), and there is an increasing recognition that the subjugation of social policy concerns to the labour market poses some risk to social order (Jordan 1998). Traditional infrastructures or 'social fabric' are compromised by the 'hollowing out of the state', and the caring networks of family and community are seen as inadequate to fill the gap subsequently created (Rodger 2000). Practically, people may not have ready access to such systems as families and communities fragment when labour forces migrate and traditional bonds are broken in late modern societies. In addition, duty and obligation to others have been weakened, either by the moral dependency and moral hazard of welfare (Giddens 1998b) or by the entrepreneurial culture of the Thatcher years. Social capital – that is, trust, civic obligation and social solidarity – does not exist in sufficient measure to replace state welfare. The generation and appropriate use of social capital, and how to promote social inclusion, have become key concerns of states emerging from traditional Keynesian welfare. This is also a question of responsibility for risk, and what the appropriate balance should be between the state, the individual and other sectors such as family and community. Without the existence of social capital can risks be effectively relocated and managed at the individual, family and community level? This raises the question of the role of civil society in welfare and risk management, a key concern of Giddens's 'dialogic democracy' and the Third Way.

Dialogic democracy and the Third Way

The Third Way is not without its critics. Indeed, Giddens himself reviews the various critiques of his position in *The Third Way and Its Critics* (2000). These criticisms range from both the right and the left. Right-wing critics present the Third Way as a 'mish-mash of already familiar ideas and policies' or as mere rhetoric devoid of intellectual or policy content (Giddens 2000: 7). Such criticisms characterize the Third Way as a pragmatic response to the failing fortunes of social democratic parties (Faux 1999), with Blair and Schroeder (1999) emphasizing the role of the state as essentially entrepreneurial, 'steering not rowing'. In essence, this is old style conservatism in a softer guise, responding to the impact of globalization through social and economic programmes designed to assist citizens to adapt to the vagaries and risks of the global market. From the left, Hall (1998) puts it in rather stark terms. The Third Way casts its citizens adrift to face risks alone, no longer underpinned by a strong welfare state. In the absence of collective social insurance for risk, citizens are reduced to an individualized fearfulness, or socially excluded through the stigma of residual, means-tested welfare. In essence, the Third Way is seen as a social and economic programme designed for secure middle England, easily challenged if economic fortunes decline (P. Ryan 1999).

In contrast, Giddens (2000: 166) proposes that his 'positive welfare' can function as a counter to the risks of globalized markets, and that 'active government' is not a 'capitulation to neoliberalism' (p. 163). He argues for a restructuring of the state and government, with the state steering economic life, and government taking an active role in the revitalization of civil society:

> Government should seek to create macro-economic stability, promote investment in education and infrastructure, contain inequality and guarantee opportunities for individual self-realization. A strong welfare system, not a minimal safety net, is a core part of this package.
>
> (Giddens 2000: 164)

While the inevitability of markets, particularly the global market, is accepted, the market is not seen as the sole answer to deficits in civil society. Ethical values for example have to be 'legitimized through democratic dialogue and sustained through public action' (p. 164). Indeed, a fully functioning civil society is seen as a vital requirement for an effective market economy. The Third Way is seen as the key mechanism for effectively linking market and state, and the social capital produced by a stable civil society – 'trust and social decency' – are seen as integral to the appropriate functioning of markets and the preservation of democracy (p. 165). Central to this proposition is the 'social contract', the notion of 'no rights without responsibilities' and the increased responsibilization of citizens (Giddens 1998b: 65). For Giddens (2000: 165) this changes the government from a regulator to a facilitator 'providing resources for citizens to assume responsibility for the consequences of what they do'. With this facilitation comes individual responsibility for the appropriate management of risk. Welfare reform is seen as essential to the creation of this new social contract, with an increased emphasis upon flexible and adaptable workforces, high knowledge and skill within the workforce and the eradication of moral hazard (Giddens 1998b).

The consequences of such supply-side policies are acknowledged; for example, 'social dumping' and social exclusion.

This approach does not imply a downgrading of the needs of those outside the labour market. They should be 'invested in' just as much as others. Positive welfare means attacking problems of dependency, isolation and lack of self-fulfilment wherever they arise.

(Giddens 2000: 166)

However, the Third Way's perceived lack of engagement with social inequality and social exclusion has continued to attract critical attention (Hall 1998, Jordan 1998). Such critics are also concerned with protection, security and safety from risks largely beyond the individual's control (for example, those arising from global markets and rapid economic change). Giddens, however, transforms this argument into an issue of positive engagement with risk by characterizing risk as innovation, opportunity and responsibility as well as merely security:

Opportunity and innovation are the positive side of risk. No one can escape risk . . . but there is a basic difference between the passive experience of risk and the active exploration of risk environments. A positive engagement with risk is a necessary component of social and economic mobilization.

(Giddens 1998b: 63)

He characterizes this as the ability to take risks in a 'productive fashion' (p. 64). This productive individualism is dependent upon two key ingredients: increased participation in civic life and a revitalized democracy. Giddens sees democracy in particular as in crisis, devoid of legitimacy and largely undemocratic and unrepresentative in its processes. He argues for a democratization of democracy which would comprise devolution, greater transparency and openness in the public sphere, value for money and leaner government, the expansion of democratic processes beyond the traditional voting process and increased inclusion of citizens in policy-making. Such revitalized democracy is based upon formal equality and rights, public discussion 'free from violence' and 'authority which is negotiated rather than given by tradition' (p. 93).

This process is to be paralleled by a re-energizing of civil society to combat civil decline and weakening social solidarity. Central to such re-energizing is the harnessing of community groups and the third or voluntary sector. Community is not merely understood as traditional communities of geographical place, but as communities of interest groups bonded together by vested interest, mutual concern and exchange. This position owes much to the work of Etzioni (1993), which emphasizes moral regeneration and responsibility as vital components of the 'good society' in which community structures are seen as central to the delivery of desired goals. Social order is seen as essential but better produced through voluntary community acts than by being imposed by the state, and individual autonomy is seen as 'bounded', restricted by relations of mutuality and obligation to others (Etzioni 1997). Etzioni's emphasis upon community rather than state, and upon responsibilities as well as rights, has had a profound impact upon approaches to welfare provision. Most notable are the notion of 'something for something' and welfare to work programmes, and the replacement of dependency with responsibility and self-efficacy. Passivity is recast as a moral evil, and failure to act is seen as morally untenable (Heron and Dwyer 1999). Being 'disadvantaged' does not exclude individuals or communities from the responsibility to contribute to the wider society. Stakeholding extends such notions to market capitalism and notions of a 'stakeholder society'. The stakeholder economy emphasizes social inclusion through economic inclusion, and the provision of rights only if responsibilities (usually labour market ones) are met. Stakeholder welfare (Field 1996; Hutton 1996) mirrors these wider concerns with moral dependency and moral decay, and stresses proactive welfare aimed at promoting opportunities rather than merely operating a safety net for personal misfortune. Social inclusion via the labour market is seen as the priority, rather than the alleviation of poverty. Social inclusion or exclusion is not a matter of poverty, it is constituted as a matter of work. Traditional welfare is depicted as morally corrosive, and newly constituted welfare is seen as essential to the promotion of self-help and the broader societal remoralization advocated by Etzioni's communitarianism.

Government is seen to have a key role in supporting local community initiatives, particularly to combat poverty and deprivation. The reduction of crime and the protection of public spaces are seen as integral to such community regeneration, the reclaiming of public spaces for civility based upon crime reduction partnerships. Quality of life is seen as central to social order, solidarity and civility. The reconstitution of family life along democratic lines is also seen as an essential ingredient of improved civil life and social order, with family essential to the maintenance of the social fabric. Family and community are seen as the key locales within which individuals will harness the resources to manage risk in an innovative and opportunistic manner.

Giddens's proposal for a supply-side positive welfare has also been critiqued on more practical and empirical grounds. Jordan, for example, notes that while equality of *opportunities* is emphasized, equality of outcomes is not necessarily achieved. As a redistributive agenda the Third Way is limited by its lack of engagement with existing power structures and its submission to the global market. Transnational redistributive issues are largely ignored or at best accepted as a given to be managed, and increasingly managed at an individual or community level. Jordan also contends that social diversity and potential conflict over scarce resources may well upset the Third Way objective of increased participation and political integration. There is perhaps a degree of naivety about the role of vested interest groups and the differential power of such groups to achieve their aims over the interests of others and the lack of regulatory power that governments can exercise over this process (for example, the disproportionate power exercised by fuel protestors in Britain and other EU countries over fuel taxes in the autumn of 2000). Jordan also doubts the ability of the labour market to deliver economic and social justice, as the labour market already has endemic injustices and inefficiencies within it. People do not enter the labour market with formally equal chances to gain and utilize the same opportunities. Post-Fordism, with its emphasis upon labour deregulation and flexibility, is likely to exacerbate this position. To some extent, supply will be driven by demand, and some workers will be more 'in demand'. Those who are surplus supply have less rights but more risks, and a weakened safety net to catch them. The social policy objective of reconstituting remoralized social actors predisposed to do the 'right thing' through a combination of inducements and retrenchment is doubted by Jordan (2000). He notes that top-down social engineering programmes have often backfired owing to perverse incentives and the unwitting poverty traps they can create. He poses Working Families Tax Credit as a key example in which claimants are reducing their working hours to the minimum level commensurate with claiming, in effect circumventing the government's work ethic in an unintended way. In this case, the notion of reciprocity is undermined by self-interest.

Taylor-Gooby *et al.* (1999; Taylor-Gooby 2000a) have explored people's perceptions of the welfare state's solutions to risk, and argue that there is still widespread support for state solutions to unforeseen risks, and to those risks which people have not been able to manage successfully. Rather than widespread disillusion with the welfare state, they found high mistrust for private insurance solutions, combined with pragmatic responses to state retrenchment and an altruistic view of welfare for those less fortunate. The contention that state welfare has no place in the risk society is challenged:

The new welfare consumers are acutely aware of their need for an extensive government-provided safety net. The annual surveys of the British Social Attitudes programme and more detailed work through EBB demonstrates that they are willing to pay higher taxes to finance it (Brook, Hall and Preston 1996: 189–90). Individual responsibility does not preclude state support and the self conscious members of a risk society are not necessarily convinced that traditional state-centred collective institutions no longer serve common interests.

(Taylor-Gooby *et al.* 1999: 192)

Rodger (2000) doubts whether contemporary societies have the social solidarity and infrastructures of caring networks to provide welfare. He cautions against the assumption that civil society can step in, and argues that the reformulation of social citizenship and social solidarity is a tough agenda. Social capital itself is not easily generated and, as Rodger puts it, 'can also be built or destroyed by structural forces beyond the control of the most community-minded citizen imaginable' (p. 186). He warns against using the global economy as an excuse for 'relinquishing collective responsibility for those unable to support themselves in an increasingly unforgiving capitalist order' (p. 187). Rodger has less faith in the potential of communitarianism than Giddens. His view of the benefits of community action and regeneration is mixed: benefits cannot necessarily be guaranteed. For Rodger social policy has yet to engage fully with the question of 'how citizens of the inner cities and peripheral housing estates are to become members of a welfare society' (p. 187). 'Self-organized welfare' may have to become a necessity in post-Fordist economies, but the Third Way is not necessarily the only way. Reciprocity, responsibility and community cannot simply be created.

While disputed by Giddens, the Third Way contains elements of Jessop's neo-liberalism mixed with neo-corporatism and some elements of neo-communitarianism. In its actual implementation under New Labour, neo-liberalism has been most evident (Powell 2000), with endeavours to formulate neo-corporate partnerships between state and business, and state and the voluntary sector. Communitarianism has been less evident beyond its occasional rhetorical use (Jordan 1998). However, social obligation and social responsibility are espoused, along with a responsibilization of the individual (for example, see Blair 1998b). For some commentators this is not necessarily about the re-energizing of civil society and increased participation and democracy. Instead, it is associated with more subtle forms of governance and regulation in advanced liberal societies.

The responsibilization of the individual and advanced liberal governance

This approach to the welfare state is most often represented in Foucauldian critiques of the role of welfare and its disciplinary techniques (Foucault 1965, 1973; Donzelot 1980; Dean 1989). Within this approach the primary function of the welfare state is not the alleviation of poverty or the reduction of social exclusion, but the identification, classification and regulation of deviant individuals and groups. The role of welfare in controlling populations and protecting existing sites of power has long been accepted (Foucault 1973, 1977, 1978), and has been seen as a central feature of welfare under modernity. In such critiques welfare agencies are recast as 'soft policing' agencies (Rodger 2000) concerned, for example, with the policing of deviant families (Donzelot 1980), and the normalization of deviant individuals towards preset norms. In this sense, welfare agencies do not solve the problems of individuals, but they constitute them and classify them in terms of deviancy from a normalized reality (Rojek *et al.* 1988). The 'psy' disciplines have been integral to the treatment of deviancy; for example, in social work, social care and offender rehabilitation, delivered through an extensive network of state-controlled agencies. Social security, far from being a universal safety net, has been characterized as 'disciplinary partitioning', a form of classifying the deserving from the indolent and for attributing moral censure to the latter (Dean 1989). The traditional welfare state was seen as integral to state regulation and integration of the individual.

However, late modernity, and for some commentators postmodernity, presents particular challenges to traditional forms of regulation and integration, resulting in 'problematics of government' and issues of governance (Burchell *et al.* 1991). These issues are most easily captured in the work of Rose (1992, 1993, 1994, 1996) and his proposition that:

> Although strategies of welfare sought to govern *through society,* 'advanced' liberal strategies of rule ask whether it is possible to govern without governing *society,* that is to say, to govern through the regulated and accountable choices of autonomous agents – citizens, consumers, parents, employees, managers, investors – and to govern through intensifying and acting upon their allegiance to particular 'communities'.
>
> (Rose 1996: 61)

This is rule at the 'molecular level', a reinvention of government in which the active citizen is required to self-regulate and such regulation is reinforced in individual and localized instances of interaction and experience. Direct state-driven controls are replaced by 'a plethora of indirect mechanisms that can translate the goals of political, social and economic authorities into the choices and commitments of individuals' (Rose 1996: 58). Social insurance as a mechanism of social solidarity is superseded. The order and control delivered by collective welfare and its disciplinary techniques is replaced by individualized risk management, self-management towards the preset prudential aims of advanced liberal societies. The state's role becomes that of facilitator and educator towards 'good' risk choices: through education, training, health campaigns etc. The 'expert' and expertise replace the state welfare worker as people purchase their own advice, counselling and support, and as self-help groups proliferate. Self-regulation of conduct becomes the key principle of government. The well educated, well advised, ethically responsible and active citizen will make the required choice. Those who do not are cast as the agents of their own misfortune. Disadvantage and exclusion are a matter of choice and not of structural processes. Such citizens are ripe for remoralization and 'ethical reconstruction as active citizens' through training, counselling, empowerment and community action (Rose 1996: 60; Cruickshank 1996). Rose (1986a, b) contends that the technologies of control are many and subtle. Embodied in daily experiences and patterns of life, or what he calls 'micro-moral domains or communities', 'The relationship between the responsible individual and their self-governing community comes to substitute for that between social citizens and their common society' (Rose 1996: 56).

The state has been replaced by the self-regulation of prudentialism and responsibilization, and by indirect mechanisms of accountability that join the subject to the state: through the market and the role of consumer, through professionals and expertise, the regulation of lifestyles through advertising (Rose 1990) and social obligations to family, workplace and neighbourhood (Rose 1996: 56–8). 'Free will' is reconstituted as making the 'right choice' (Miller and Rose 1990; Petersen and Lupton 1996). Governmentality – that is, regulating conduct – is displaced to the micro domain of individual and locale, with the residual role of welfare agencies constituted as facilitating prudential choices through the provision of expert knowledge and in the provision of 'rational choices' for the individual (e.g. public health campaigns).

Advanced liberal forms of welfare and the accompanying social policy of responsibilization have been characterized as a response to the indeterminancy and deregulation of the risk society. Diversity and pluralism threaten social solidarity, and modernist forms of state-centred coercive control (no matter how subtly delivered by the 'psy' disciplines of welfare) are increasingly costly and unwieldy (Turner 1997). Displacement to the reconstituted free will of the individual is seen as more effective and efficient (Miller and Rose 1990). However, whether the 'social' has truly ended and is entirely replaced by individual self-regulation is a contested point, and welfare provision at present is probably more easily characterized as a mixture of modern social insurance and individual prudentialism (Kelly and Charlton 1995).

Postmodern welfare

Advanced liberal characterizations of the state and of the place of welfare and social policy within it owe much to postmodern considerations (Carter 1998). While postmodern welfare and social policy has its doubters (Carter 1998), there is a recognition that the impact of globalization in particular and the 'end of certainty' (Leonard 1997) has led to welfare in 'new times' and that 'Fabian conceptions of governance are accordingly outdated and the state itself should be seen as "disconnected and erratic" (Hillyard and Watson 1996: 338)' (Carter 1998: 22). Leonard (1997) has outlined a postmodern programme of welfare. He contends that the social democratic discourse of welfare, based upon Fabian notions of incremental change characterized by Titmuss's (1968) moral progressive programme of social policy and welfare, has been severely challenged by globalization, discontinuities and the cultural uncertainty of postmodernity. For Leonard the 'past is another country' and the present is an uncertain place (pp. 23, 25). While the global market is a universal, 'it touches, through technology, cultural production and increasing market dependency, virtually all of humanity' (p. 25); its impact for Leonard is to create an 'Other' excluded from the global market:

> The Other is, by definition, diverse, fragmented, excluded and so its multifarious component populations cannot separately empower themselves to oppose the massive power of the new market forces of subordination, exploitation and homogenisation.
>
> (Leonard 1997: 27)

The diversity of postmodernity paradoxically feeds the global market by creating ever more diverse needs to be met, but it also creates issues for welfare and for governance: how to govern and regulate the diverse range of excluded groups; how to deal with the plethora of risks. Markets require diversity but also homogeneity, diverse needs but social stability. The discourse of modernity is characterized by 'liberal, humanistic individualism' in which the universal subject is presumed, and difference, the identification of different and excluded others, is a major preoccupation of modernity's knowledge and institutional practices (Leonard 1997: 49). For Leonard, the subjects of the welfare state have long been constituted by such binary discourse: self–other, included–excluded, with the most powerful division 'between the subject as dependent and independent' (p. 50). Leonard identifies a significant shift in this division, particularly under New Right political regimes, from dependence upon the state (epitomized by the rhetoric of the 'underclass': Murray 1990), to independence via the labour market (or, as Leonard puts it, 'market dependency'). Individuals are doubly bonded to the market: by being consumers and by being wage earners.

Order in a world of diversity is achieved through increased mechanisms of 'self-surveillance'. While the 'professions of welfare' exercised 'disciplinary power' in modernity (Leonard 1997: 55), within postmodernity self-surveillance is pursued as a more 'efficient and cost-effective form of control' (Foucault 1991; Leonard 1997: 56). This self-surveillance is achieved through the discourse of expertise, through the discourse of moral virtue and 'rational choice' experienced by the individual as an autonomous form of control – in essence, through the governance techniques of advanced liberal societies. A key mechanism of this self-surveillance is self-disclosure, the postmodern version of Western Christianity's confessional. Such disclosure is seen as the first step in reconstituting the self as a new, remoralized individual subjugated to the instructions of professional expertise. Seeking help, dealing with one's problems, changing one's anti-social thinking patterns, engaging in self-help and adapting healthier lifestyles are all part of this reconstituting self-surveillance: 'Thus, the state in late capitalism is able, through the discourses and practices of self-regulation, to continue the exercise of power, but as Foucault maintained, in an increasingly economical way' (Leonard 1997: 59).

However, Leonard sees this transition as a source of other possibilities: the future is undetermined. He contends that the myth of independence will be challenged by the uncertainties and fragmentation caused by the impact of the global market. Deregulation of labour markets, for example, and the demand for increased flexibility create uncertainty for individuals in the labour market and risks that are beyond their ability to influence or control. Dependency upon the labour market is a tenuous one, and citizens may recognize the threat of increased individualization contained within advanced liberalism. For Leonard the high risks of labour market dependency may enable individuals to recognize the importance of interdependence with others. Indeed, he argues that some self-disclosure and self-reconstitution is done in groups and serves a largely emancipatory agenda (for example, feminism) or creates sites of power and opposition to governmental forms (groups contesting oppressive power relationships, for example). Harris (1999) has also contended that occupational and fiscal welfare, while apparently more easily characterized by a self-actualizing discourse, have actually been the subject of numerous collective actions. The collective bargaining of unionization, which extended beyond wage packets to sickness benefits and health programmes, pressure groups and vested interest groups in the realm of fiscal welfare (the pensioner power increasingly exerted over pensions, fuel protestors, the farming lobby) and claimants' groups in the area of public welfare (for example, disability groups) are key examples.

Thompson and Hoggett (1996) have argued that the polarization between universalism and selectivism highlighted within postmodern analyses of welfare is unhelpful. They contend that contemporary social policy should combine universalism with particularism; that is, universal principles of provision combined with specificity in terms of concrete delivery. Such combined provision can protect rights, needs and entitlements on the one hand, and offer diversity, equality and relevance to users on the other. Thompson and Hoggett (1996: 38) argue that this form of welfare can be delivered through state residual welfare of 'basic welfare needs', with 'specific welfare needs' delivered through local, devolved 'voluntary self-governing associations' – in essence, a combined system of centralized residual state provision and specific, flexible provision at the devolved local level. However, how this hybrid would actually operate in a climate of differing vested interest groups is left largely undeveloped. While conceptually particularism can be posed as a positive substitute for selectivism, its practical implementation and management in social policy-making requires more thought.

While postmodern and largely Foucauldian analyses of welfare have been useful for focusing attention on issues of governance and the 'social', the extent to which welfare in all its various forms can be located as postmodern is questioned (Carter 1998, 1999). In particular, such analyses have been criticized for a narrow focus on state, bureaucratic welfare provision, with little emphasis upon other welfare forms such as 'fiscal welfare' through taxation and 'occupational welfare' through employment (Titmuss 1963; Carter 1998). Indeed, it is possible to understand advanced liberal welfare forms as a shift from public welfare to occupational welfare supported in part by additions to the fiscal welfare system.

The attention to 'public welfare' is justified by some commentators because its concern with populations defined as dependent 'is problematic for liberal governance' (Harris 1999: 29). Welfare to dependent populations necessarily raises issues of the appropriate balance between dependency/assistance and autonomy/self-governance. For Harris this places liberal government on the 'horns of a dilemma': assistance may be required to get people back into market place productivity, but assistance might undermine market processes, create moral hazard and undermine processes of self-regulation. Harris argues that the governmentality literature examines key shifts in the balance between dependence and independence, state intervention and self-regulation – in essence, key shifts in Western forms of governance. Such shifts are seen as particularly acute at the present time because of the demise of modernity and the transition into late modernity or postmodernity. Modern governmentality is characterized by Foucault as a specific form of power which utilizes a political economy of knowledge targeted at the population, governing through 'the welfare of the population, the improvement of its condition, the increase of wealth, longevity, health etc.' (Foucault 1991: 100).

The role of postmodern analysis in social policy and welfare debates has been to render these mechanisms of governance transparent, and to plot the key shifts in their form and application. Of particular importance has been the identification of excluded groups, particularly the potential for new groups not constituted on traditional class and gender lines, and the potential for a fragmented citizenry (Harris 1999). This fragmented citizenry has been characterized as a shift from citizenship 'construed in terms of solidarity, welfare and security' (Miller and Rose 1988: 24), towards citizenship construed in terms of 'self-help and individual enterprise' (Harris 1999: 46). Formal contracts and an exchange economy characterize citizenship, and distinctions between those in the market (either as consumers or as workers) are marked. As discussed above, whether this has resulted in the 'death of the social' (Rose 1996) is contested. Rodger (2000) and Giddens (1998b), for example, have drawn attention to active social domains in the voluntary sector and at local and community level. This may amount to a reconfiguration of the social but not necessarily to its death. However, what is clear in advanced liberalism is the 'subordination of mutuality to contractual relations' (Harris 1999: 46). For Harris this means that the 'fragmentation of the social' endangers citizenship because those dependent upon residual public welfare are seen as deficient and blameworthy. While there is nothing new in the moral stigma of welfare, the constitution of citizenship as entirely economic is. This narrows opportunities for participation and citizenship, and in effect excludes large segments of the population from full and active citizenship.

However, Harris (1999: 49) sees possibilities for resistance and change within the markertization and contractual configuration of welfare, an area of 'contestation'. Civil rights lobbyists contest the erosion of individual liberty and the growth of surveillance; pensioners and the disability movement contest the inadequacies and residualism of state welfare; minority groups contest the inequality of income. Advanced liberalism finds itself critiqued on the grounds of social exclusion and social instability (Hutton 1996). The increased preoccupation with governance and its shifting forms itself allows for other formulations of governance, social policy and welfare to be explored. Harris sees one possible route in the deconstruction of the powerful dichotomy of work and welfare and its attendant eligibility criteria, and an increased emphasis upon the mutuality of all citizens. This would remove income from the realms of the market in which it would always have to be earned, to the realms of citizenry and public welfare, guaranteed to provide active citizenship and social inclusion.

Leonard (1997: 162) also sees a 'politics of hope' arising from these 'new times', in which human welfare is reconstructed as an 'emancipatory project'. By drawing on the critiques of modern welfare posed by feminism and Marxism, Leonard outlines the possibility of a diverse and critical subject constituted as a 'resistant moral agent' for whom the totalizing and homogeneous forms of traditional welfare are no longer acceptable. New welfare

> cannot be based upon some overall grand plan . . . because the over-ambitious planning, programming and organization of welfare institutions . . . produced the paradox that a commitment to welfare resulted . . . in a system of domination in the interests of exclusion, homogenization and the defence of expert power.
>
> (Leonard 1997: 163)

Leonard sees the *process* of delivery and not planning as the key to meeting diverse needs. This requires the resolution of two key tensions in postmodernity: the promotion and acceptance of difference without compromising social solidarity and the promotion of a negative and excluding individualism. This tension is most easily expressed in the construction and delivery of ethnically and culturally sensitive services without compounding issues of exclusion and oppression. As Leonard (1997: 65) expresses it,

> The danger of an unrestrained emphasis upon difference is that it will lead to cultural exclusiveness, restricted identities or intense indi-

vidualism. The comparable danger of a triumphant and unreflecting solidarity is that domination and homogenization become a practice legitimated by a discourse on mutual interdependence.

Leonard proposes that a discourse of mutual interdependency can be wisely used to counter the late modern trend of an individualized discourse of welfare dependency. As the negative impacts of the increased individualization of welfare are felt and become a common experience across a range of groups and individuals, the 'potential solidarity between the individual subjects of welfare' is fostered (Leonard 1997: 166). As with Harris, this is seen as a site of potential resistance. In essence, Leonard articulates a two-tier welfare state in which 'common human needs' would be met by the state, and more culturally specific ones by those who articulate them. However, in the latter arena the state may need to be the final arbiter of what level and expression of difference are acceptable, so that the least powerful (for example, children) are protected. Thus, new welfare cannot avoid moral judgements any more than 'old' welfare could. In essence, the role of the state as the manager of vested interests is more pronounced and perhaps more transparent, but whether the state will have either the power or the long-term integrity to manage vested interest in the face of the economic and cultural power of capital is a moot point. The appropriate protection of the weak in a federation of diverse vested interest groups remains a difficult issue, only partially resolved by Leonard's reflective welfare professionals and welfare building without the worst excesses of repression, surveillance and control. As he states, welfare reconstruction is itself subject to state control, and 'can the state be trusted?' (p. 175). While disenchantment with the political process is now commonplace, and the argument for a 'confederation of diversities' to replace traditional political parties is attractive, whether the 'challenge' and hence the transformation of state form will take place is a question that 'cannot be answered at this point' (p. 178). While Leonard is clear that the requirement to change is very real, the actual likelihood of transformation and of its precise mechanisms is less clear. As Rodger states, this is the key challenge for postmodern societies: how to accommodate varying interests in the policy process and at the same time reduce the overtly controlling role of the state without risking chaos.

Summary

In the shifting sands of British welfare provision at the start of the twenty-first century a number of key positions can be discerned among social policy commentators. Most notable are Jessop's Schumpterian workfare state, Giddens's dialogic democracy, Rose's advanced liberal governance and postmodern welfare analyses. While there are distinct features within each position, some key trends can be discerned. Particularly, these are changes in the relationship between the individual and the state, changes in patterns and strategies of governance, welfare residualism in the face of high costs and global markets, and concerns with the economic maintenance of social order and civil society. These are among the key issues facing welfare states in the coming century and the social policy choices about their resolution will characterize the future of welfare provision.

The implications for welfare workers: the new risk orthodoxy

Welfare workers in the twenty-first century find themselves part of a new residualism of welfarism within which risk plays a key part in resource allocation and in the framing of their professional practice and encounters with service users. Their professional world is characterized by key themes: fiscal prudence, rationing, risk assessment, targeting and responsibilization of service users. The top-down social engineering of the Third Way is mirrored in the top-down managerialism exerted in all aspects of health and social care. The increasing residualism of welfare is mirrored in the distancing of workers from users, particularly in social care, combined with increasingly formal techniques of assessment to ensure appropriate and consistent targeting. Assessment is no longer needs-led but is concerned with checking eligibility; assessments are in effect the key mechanism through which harsh gatekeeping is exercised. In child protection, for example, this has resulted in an explosion of investigative assessments but a reduction in preventative or long-term work with families. Classification and categorization of users, most usually in terms of risk or vulnerability, has become a central task for workers, often implemented using highly prescriptive guidelines and formalized risk assessment tools (Kemshall *et al.* 1997). Alaszewski (2000: 11) has argued that this could result in a 'dark age of risk':

> The 1990s can be characterised in health and welfare services as the risk decade. If risk is defined in a narrow technical fashion as threat and danger, then agencies and professionals will be forced to act as technocratic hazard managers, and in the process will disempower vulnerable service users.

Such disempowerment of users is most easily found in their objectification as cases, with case management ensuring management and fiscal control through the use of pre-specified packages. For workers, social care provision is no longer about individual needs assessment and professional judgement about interventions, it is about matching eligible users to predetermined outcomes. The latter increasingly reflect the dual concerns of contemporary welfare, the remoralization of social actors and civil society and the displacement of risk management through responsibilization. This is Jordan's 'tough love' *par excellence*: welfare as a moral enterprise and workers too are part of this new moral enterprise. Key techniques in the remoralization of the workforce are the spectre of blame and self-management through the forensic functions of risk and its attendant systems of audit and accountability (Kemshall *et al.* 1997). These are paralleled by 'evidence-based' interventions usually rooted in the discipline of psychology and cognitive–behavioural techniques of change. The emphasis of such techniques is 'self-change', 'straight thinking', 'rational choices', with the users made responsible for both their own problems and their solution. Interventions tend towards the didactic, premised on appropriate information giving, instruction, sanctions, enforcement and inducement to make the 'correct choice'. Those who fail to do so run the risk of having their eligibility reassessed or are confronted with compulsory correction or exclusion (for example, prison or mental health detention). Workers too are subject to 'straight thinking'; for example, in compulsory training in the techniques and subsequent testing of psychological suitability to implement them, in evaluations of their 'programme integrity' and in audits of risk assessments. Technique is valued above judgement or reflection (Kemshall 2000), and tools are used to replace the vagaries of clinical judgement.

Summary

Welfare workers in the twenty-first century are likely to continue to face rapid change as welfare is subjected to considerable reframing, in terms of both its objectives and its methods of delivery. No area of welfare will be immune. The trends in the practice and management of welfare services are already clear. Markets, partnership, prudence and residualism have all impacted upon the organization and management of welfare delivery, and practice has been reconstructed as a largely risk-led, technical enterprise.

The rise of risk and the end of welfare

As Powell and Hewitt (1998: 1), express it, the demise of the welfare state may be premature, and that while it 'is being redefined . . . reports of its death have been much exaggerated'. While the debate about the level of consensus or otherwise on the fate and definition of twenty-first-century welfare is alive and well and the future of welfare is highly contested (Powell 2000), key trends can be identified:

- universalism is no longer a cornerstone principle;
- residualism, targeting and selectivity are accepted;
- mixed provision is promoted;

- responsibilization is the price of citizenship and inclusion;
- social inclusion is dependent upon engagement with and role in the labour market;
- individuals and their communities are increasingly responsible for the generation and prudent use of their own welfare resources (active rather than passive welfare);
- central to prudentialism is self-assessment and self-management of risk.

Within these trends it is possible to identify both significant continuities with previous New Right policies and welfare forms embedded within modernity (Powell 2000), and emerging forms and discontinuities (Leonard 1997; Harris 1999). However, one clear unifying theme is risk, and the differing approaches to it adopted by social policy and welfare regimes over time. As Taylor-Gooby (2000b: 3) paradoxically points out, at a time of greatest material security people are highly anxious about risks, a 'growing uncertainty amid rising mass affluence'. With the considerable benefit of hindsight the welfare recipient of the twentieth century has been recast as either risk-adverse (preferring welfare dependency) or an imprudent risk taker (taking risks with self, health and future prosperity). The welfare recipient of the twenty-first century has been cast as a largely residual category replaced where possible by the responsible risk-taking citizen prudently exercising a range of risk choices. While welfare restructuring is incomplete and the final outcome of present transformations is as yet unknown, there can be little doubt about the role of risk in British social policy and welfare provision, whether this be the collective risks of Beveridge welfare insurance and social solidarity, the moral hazards and risks of dependency of Thatcherism or the opportunity risks and prudentialism of advanced liberal governance. Welfare regimes have been constructed and deployed to deal with risk and to deliver key social policy objectives on societal risk management. The techniques, strategies and mechanisms may have changed with the times, and the objectives may have been reconstituted from social solidarity, to control and discipline, to diversity management. The risks too have changed, as have our perception and anxiety about them, and more importantly so has the locus of responsibility for risk taking and risk management. Whatever the form of welfare provision adopted by Britain in the twenty-first century, a central issue will be the equitable distribution of risks and of social and individual resources to bear and manage them. In this sense, risk will continue to be the central issue for welfare in the twenty-first century.

Note

1 This concept is discussed in more detail in Chapter 1 of this volume.

Suggestions for further reading

Lewis, G., Gewirtz, S. and Clarke, J. (2000) *Rethinking Social Policy*. London: Sage. This edited work addresses contemporary trends in social policy and the changing face of welfare. Chapters 4 and 11 are particularly helpful.

Taylor-Gooby, P. (2000) *Risk, Trust and Welfare*. Basingstoke: Macmillan Press. This edited work relinks issues in current social policy developments to risk in contemporary society. A key strength of the book is its use of recent empirical research by the contributors, and Chapters 1, 2, 4, 5 and 10 are particularly useful.

Glossary

Advanced liberalism a term describing a mode of governing associated with the emergence of globalization and postmodern societies. The key characteristic of advanced liberal societies is the displacement of the mechanisms of government from the state to the individual, and power is exercised through the 'regulated choices' of individuals and the communities within which they are located.

Discourse describes a bounded body of knowledge that circumscribes our understanding of the world, both the natural world and social processes. Discourse defines both 'problems' and our understanding of and solutions to them. Discourse also delimits the possibilities of what can be known, and as such is about relations of power, particularly when institutionalized and embedded in social practices and organizational forms.

Fordism describes a mode of social regulation and industrial production common in Western capitalist societies in the twentieth century, characterized by mass production processes and mass consumption, rooted in Keynesian welfare states. These states are characterized by social cohesion and a mode of social regulation that supports and legitimates capitalist production and consumption.

Globalization a term describing the impact of global events, information exchange and capital upon nation states and local communities.

Governance refers to the mechanisms of governing, i.e. of achieving social control and order through the deployment of subtle techniques of power and institutionalized discursive practices rather than the use of overt state coercion. The major technique of governance in advanced liberal societies is self-regulation through a discourse of risk and prudentialism and the use of expert knowledge to guide the activities and choices of the 'prudential citizen'.

Governmentality refers to the system of governance in use, i.e. how individual conduct is regulated. In advanced liberal societies governmentality is displaced to the micro-domain of individual and locale, with the residual role of welfare agencies constituted as facilitating prudential choices through the provision of expert knowledge and in the provision of 'rational choices' for the individual (e.g. public health campaigns).

Late modernity most often associated with the work of Giddens and his analyses of social transformation at the close of the twentieth century. Globalization and the emergence of new and internally produced risks are key features of the late modernity thesis, with implications for relationships of trust as traditional social bonds weaken.

Modernity most commonly defined as the period of industrialization and capitalist expansion from the industrial revolution to the late 1970s in Western societies. The period is characterized by capitalist expansion, imperialism, representative democracies and the formulation of the welfare state.

Post-Fordism describes the emerging mode of production and social regulation in late modern industrial societies. Post-Fordist states are characterized by flexible labour markets and production, technological innovation, economic regulation based upon flexibility and enterprise, lean organizational forms and flexible supply.

Postmodernity describes the period from the late 1970s onwards and the social transformations emerging at the start of the twenty-first century. Postmodernity is characterized by global risks, indeterminate and contingent knowledge about the probability of such risks and uncertainty over future outcomes and impacts. The distinction between late modernity and postmodernity is most often expressed in terms of the impact of globalization, and the degree of uncertainty and pluralism detected in cultural forms.

Prudentialism requires the citizen to adopt a calculating attitude towards almost all of his or her decisions. Thus the individual becomes the primary site of risk management, not society, and the 'good' citizen is the responsible, prudential one. Prudentialism is most often associated with mechanisms of governance in advanced liberal societies.

Reflexivity a term most usually associated with the work of Giddens, describing a key characteristic of life in post-traditional societies. The 'risk society' presents the individual with a myriad of risks, many of which are uncertain in nature. The individual therefore must constantly self-monitor risk decisions and risk choices.

Responsibilization a term describing a form of governance dependent upon what Rose (2000) has described as 'responsibilization'; that is, individuals are made responsible for their own actions, including their own risks, and for their own effective self-management.

Risk society most often associated with the work of Beck and Giddens, and rooted in their analysis of late modern society and the social transformations impacting upon capitalist modes of production, modes of social regulation and traditional social bonds. A key feature of such transformations is the internal production of risks, often globally located but individually experienced. The dominant culture is one of fearfulness and a precautionary principle based upon a desire for safety.

Third Way refers to a framework of thinking and policy-making that seeks to adapt social democracy to a world challenged by global markets and global risks. The political programme aims to transcend both traditional social democracy and New Right neo-liberalism. The following key strands can be identified in the Third Way: social responsibility and obligations, the use of the labour market to achieve social justice, emphasis upon meritocracy, residual welfare and targeting, and modernization.

Bibliography

Acheson, D. (Chair) (1998) *Independent Inquiry into Inequalities in Health Report*. London: The Stationery Office.

Adams, J. (1995) *Risk*. London: UCL Press.

Age Concern (2000) *The Millennium Debate of the Age* (http://www.ace.org.co.uk).

Aharoni, Y. (1981) *The no-risk society*. Chatham, NJ: Chatham House.

Alaszewski, A. (2000) Balancing act, *Openmind*, 101 (Jan./Feb.), 10–11.

Alaszewski, A., Harrison, L. and Manthorpe, J. (eds) (1998) *Risk, Health and Welfare*. Buckingham: Open University Press.

Albertsen, N. (1988) Postmodernism, post-Fordism and critical social theory, *Environment and Planning D: Society and Space*, 6, 339–65.

Aldgate, J., Tunstill, J. and McBeath, G. (1992) *National Monitoring of the Children Act: Part III Section 17 – The First Year*. Oxford: Oxford University/NCVCCO.

Allandale, E. (1998) *The Sociology of Health and Medicine: A Critical Introduction*. Cambridge: Polity Press.

Allsop, J. (1995) *Health Policy and the NHS: Towards 2000*, 2nd edn. London: Longman.

Allsop, J. (1997) Why health care should be provided free at the point of service, in D. Gladstone (ed.) *How to Pay for Health Care: Public and Private Alternatives*. London: The IEA Health and Welfare Unit.

Aries, P. (1962) *Centuries of Childhood*. Harmondsworth: Penguin.

Association of British Insurers (1995) *Risk, Insurance and Welfare: The Changing Balance between Public and Private Protection*. London: The Association of British Insurers.

Audit Commission (1986) *Making a Reality of Community Care*. London: HMSO.

Audit Commission (1992) *The Community Revolution: The Personal Social Services and Community Care*. London: HMSO.

Audit Commission (1994a) *Seen but Not Heard: Co-ordinating Child Health and Social Services for Children in Need*. London: HMSO.

Audit Commission (1994b) *Finding a Place: A Review of Mental Health Services for Adults*. London: HMSO.

Audit Commission (1997) *The Coming of Age: Improving Care Services for Older People*. London: Audit Commission.

Baggott, R. (1998) *Health and Health Care in Britain*. Basingstoke: St Martin's Press.

Baldock, J. (1994) The personal social services: the politics of care, in V. George and S. Miller (eds) *Social Policy towards 2000: Squaring the Welfare Circle*. London: Routledge.

Barclay (1982) *Social Workers: Their Role and Tasks* (The Barclay Report). Report for the government produced by the National Institute for Social Work, Bedford Square Press.

Barham, P. and Hayward, R. (1991) *From Mental Patient to Person*. London: Routledge.

Barkham, P. (2000) The NHS, *Guardian* website, 5 May (www.guardianunlimited. co.uk/NHS).

Barr, N. (1992) *The Economics of the Welfare State*, 2nd edn. London: Weidenfeld and Nicholson.

Barry, N. (1990) *Welfare*. Buckingham: Open University Press.

Bartlett, P. (1997) *Closing the Asylum: The Mental Patient in Modern Society*, 2nd edn. Harmondsworth: Penguin.

Bartlett, P. and Sandland, R. (2000) *Mental Health Law: Policy and Practice*. London: Blackstone Press Ltd.

Bartlett, P. and Wright, D. (1999) *Outside the Walls of the Asylum: The History of Care in the Community 1730–2000*. London: Athlone.

BBC (2000a) Pensioner power: the new old protesters? 21 September (www.news. bbc.co.uk).

BBC (2000b) Poverty spreads among the UK's elderly. 21 September (www.news. bbc.co.uk).

Beck, U. (1992a) *Risk Society: Towards a New Modernity*. London: Sage.

Beck, U. (1992b) From industrial society to the risk society: questions of survival, social structure and ecological enlightenment, *Theory, Culture and Society*, 1 (February), 97–123.

Beck, U. (1996) Risk society and the provident state, in S. Lash, B. Szerzinski and B. Wynne (eds) *Risk, Environment and Modernity: Towards a New Ecology*. London: Sage.

Beck, U. (1998) Politics of risk society, in J. Franklin (ed.) *The Politics of Risk Society*. Cambridge: Polity Press in association with the Institute for Public Policy Press.

Bellaby, P. (1990) To risk or not to risk? Uses and limitations of Mary Douglas on risk acceptability for understanding health and safety at work and road accidents, *Sociological Review*, 30(3), 465–83.

Bernstein, P. L. (1996) *Against the Gods: The Remarkable Story of Risk*. New York: John Wiley.

Beveridge, W. (1942) *Social Insurance and Allied Services*, Cmd 6404. London: HSMO.

Bingley, W. (1997) Assessing dangerousness: protecting the interest of patients, *British Journal of Psychiatry*, 170 (Supplement 32), 28–9.

Black, D., Morris, J., Smith, C. and Townsend, P. (1980) *Inequalities in Health Care*. London: HMSO.

Blair, T. (1993) Extract from speech given by Tony Blair MP to Wellingborough Constituency Party, 3 March. News Release, The Labour Party, 150 Walworth Road, London.

Blair, T. (1997) Speech at Durham, 22 December (available via http://www.labour.org.uk).

Blair, T. (1998a) Interview, on *Breakfast with Frost*, ITV, 11 January.

Blair, T. (1998b) *The Third Way*. London: The Fabian Society.

Blair, T. (2000a) Blair's vision for the NHS: full text of the speech at St Thomas' Hospital, London (www.guardianunlimited.co.uk/NHS).

Blair, T. (2000b) *National Plan for the NHS*. House of Commons, 27 July.

Blair, T. and Schroeder, G. (1999) *Europe: The Third Way/Die Neue Mitte*. A joint declaration by Tony Blair and Gerhard Schroeder, London, 8 June (available via http://www.labour.org.uk).

Blanks, R. G., Moss, S. M., McGahan, E., Quinn, M. J. and Babb, P. J. (2000) Effect of NHS breast screening programme on mortality from breast cancer in England and Wales, 1990–1998: comparison of observed with predicted mortality, *British Medical Journal*, 321, 665–9.

Blom-Cooper, L. (1996) *The Case of Jason Mitchell: Report of the Independent Panel of Inquiry*. London: Duckworth.

Blom-Cooper, L., Hally, H. and Murphy, E. (1995) *The Falling Shadow: One Patient's Mental Health Care 1978–1993*. London: Gerald Duckworth and Co.

Bloor, M. (1995) *The Sociology of HIV Transmission*. London: Sage.

Bourlet, J. (1994) *Rationing and the Future of UK Health Care*. London: Independent Health Association.

Bowlby, J. (1951) *Maternal Care and Mental Health*. A report prepared on behalf of the World Health Organization as a contribution to the United Nations programme for the welfare of homeless children. Geneva: World Health Organization.

Boyd Report (1996) *Report of the Confidential Inquiry into Homicides and Suicides by Mentally Ill People*. Steering Committee of the Confidential Inquiry. London: Royal College of Psychiatrists.

Bradshaw, J. (1972) The concept of social need, *New Society*, 30 March, 640–3.

Bradshaw, J. (1994) The conceptualization and measurement of need. A social policy perspective, in J. Popay and G. Williams (eds) *Researching People's Health*. London: Routledge.

Braye, S. and Preston-Shoot, M. (1995) *Empowering Practice in Social Care*. Buckingham: Open University Press.

Brewer, C. and Lait, J. (1980) *Can Social Work Survive?* London: Temple Smith.

Brindle, D. (1996) NHS to sell private care plans, *Guardian*, 25 March.

Brook, L., Hall, J. and Preston, I. (1996) Public spending and taxation, in R. Jowell (ed.) *1996 British Social Attitudes*. Aldershot: Dartmouth.

Brown, C. (2000) Comment on NHS proposals, *PM Programme*, BBC Radio 4, 31 May.

Brown, H. and Smith, H. (1992) *Normalisation: A Reader for the Nineties*. London: Routledge.

Brown, T. (2000) AIDS, risk and social governance, *Social Science and Medicine*, 50, 1273–84.

Browne, M. (1996) Needs assessment and community care, in J. Percy-Smith (ed.) *Needs Assessment in Public Policy*. Buckingham: Open University Press.

Bunton, R. (1997) Popular health, advanced liberalism and *Good Housekeeping* magazine, in A. Petersen. and R. Bunton (eds) *Foucault, Health and Medicine*. London: Routledge.

Bunton, R., Nettleton, S. and Burrows, R. (1995) *The Sociology of Health Promotion*. London: Routledge.

Burchell, G., Gordon, C. and Miller, P. (eds) (1991) *The Foucault Effect: Studies in Governmentality*. London: Harvester Wheatsheaf.

Burrows, R. and Loader, B. (eds) (1994) *Towards a Post-Fordist Welfare State?* London: Routledge.

Butler-Schloss, E. (1988) *Report of the Inquiry into Child Abuse in Cleveland 1987*. Presented to the Secretary of State for Social Services by the Right Honourable Lord Butler-Schloss DBE. London: HMSO.

Carpenter, M. (2000) 'It's a small world': mental health policy under welfare capitalism since 1945, *Sociology of Health and Illness*, 22(5), 602–20.

Carson, D. (1988) Taking risks with your patients – your assessment strategy, *Professional Nurse*, 3(7), 247–50.

Carson, D. (1990) Risk-taking in mental disorder, in D. Carson (ed.) *Risk-taking in Mental Disorder: Analyses, Policies and Practical Strategies*. Chichester: SLE Publications.

Carson, D. (1994) Presenting risk options, *Inside Psychology*, 1(1), 3–7.

Carson, D. (1996) Risking legal repercussions, in H. Kemshall and J. Pritchard (eds) *Good Practice in Risk Assessment and Risk Management, Volume 1*. London: Jessica Kingsley Publishers.

Carter, J. (1998) Studying social policy after modernity, in J. Carter (ed.) *Postmodernity and the fragmentation of welfare*. London: Routledge.

Carter, J. (1999) Postmodernity and welfare: when worlds collide, *Social Policy and Administration*, 32(2), 101–15.

Castel, R. (1991) From dangerousness to risk, in G. Burchell, C. Gordon and P. Miller (eds) *The Foucault Effect: Studies in Governmentality*. London: Harvester Wheatsheaf.

Cavadino, P. (1999) Diverting mentally disordered offenders from custody, in D. Webb and R. Harris (eds) *Mentally Disordered Offenders: Managing People Nobody Owns*. London: Routledge.

Cervi, B. (1996) Tax payers 'subsidise' NHS pay beds, *Health Service Journal*, 3, 5 October.

Challis, D. (1992) Providing alternatives to long stay hospital care for frail elderly patients: is it cost effective? *International Journal of Geriatric Psychiatry*, 7, 773–81.

Challis, D. and Davies, B. (1986) *Case Management in Community Care*. Aldershot: Gower.

Cheetham, J. (1993) Social work and community care in the 1990s: pitfalls and potential, in R. Page and J. Baldock (eds) *Social Policy Review 5*. Canterbury: Social Policy Association.

Clark, G., Hockley, T. and Smedley, I. (1995) The insurance of medical risks, in Association of British Insurers, *Risk, Insurance and Welfare: The Changing Balance between Public and Private Protection*. London: Association of British Insurers.

Clarke, J. (1996) The problem of the state after the welfare state, in M. May,

E. Brunsdon and G. Craig (eds) *Social Policy Review 8*. London: Social Policy Association.

Clarke, J. (1999) Whose business? Social welfare and managerial calculation, in M. Purdy and D. Banks (eds) *Health and Exclusion*. London: Routledge.

Clarke, J., Cochrane, A. and McLaughlin, E. (eds) (1994) *Managing Social Policy*. London: Sage.

Clarke, J. and Newman, J. (1997) *The Managerial State*. London: Sage.

Cochrane, A. (1993) Challenges from the centre, in J. Clarke (ed.) *A Crisis in Care? Challenges to Social Work*. London: Sage in association with the Open University.

Cochrane, A. (1994) Restructuring the local welfare state, in R. Burrows and B. Loader (eds) *Towards a Post-Fordist Welfare State?* London: Routledge.

Collingbridge, S. (1992) *The Management of Scale: Big Organisations, Big Decisions, Big Mistakes*. London: Routledge.

Collingbridge, S. (1996) Resilience, flexibility and diversity in managing the risks of technologies, in C. Hood and D. K. C. Jones (eds) *Accident and Design: Contemporary Debates in Risk Management*. London: UCL Press.

Colton, M., Drury, C. and Williams, M. (1995) Children in need: definition, identification and support, *British Journal of Social Work*, 25, 711–28.

Commission for Social Justice (1994) *Social Justice – Strategies for National Renewal*. London: Vintage.

Community Care (1995) Age of independence, *Community Care*, 20–26 July, 20–1.

Community Care (1996) Snap decision, *Community Care*, 2–8 May, 31–2.

Comprehensive Spending Review (1998) *Comprehensive Spending Review*, CM 4315 London: Treasury Office.

Copas, J. B., Marshall, P. and Tarling, R. (1996) *Predicting Re-offending for Discretionary Conditional Release*. Home Office Research Study 150. London: HMSO.

Corby, B. (1993) *Child Abuse: Towards a Knowledge Base*. Buckingham: Open University Press.

Crawford, R. (1994) The boundaries of self and the unhealthy other: reflections on health, culture and AIDS, *Social Science Medicine*, 38(10), 1347–65.

Cruickshank, B. (1996) Revolutions within: self-government and self-esteem, in A. Barry, T. Osborne and N. Rose (1996) *Foucault and Political Reason: Liberalism, Neo-liberalism and Rationalities of Government*. London: UCL Press.

Cullen, Lord (1990) *The Public Inquiry into the Piper Alpha Disaster*. London: HMSO.

Culpitt, I. (1999) *Social Policy and Risk*. London: Sage.

Culyer, A. J. and Wagstaff, A. (1992) *Need Equity and Equality in Health Care*. University of York discussion paper 95.

Daily Telegraph (1997) R. Uhlig: the beef crisis – why dicing with death isn't on the menu, *Daily Telegraph*, 5 December, 9.

Daston, L. (1987) The domestication of risk: mathematical probability and insurance 1650–1830, in L. Kruger, L. Daston and M. Heidelberger (eds) *The Probabilistic Revolution. Volume 1, Ideas in History*. Cambridge, MA: MIT Press.

Davis, A. (1996) Risk work and mental health, in H. Kemshall and J. Pritchard (eds) *Good Practice in Risk Assessment and Risk Management, Volume 1*. London: Jessica Kingsley Publishers.

Davies, C. (2000) The demise of professional self-regulation: a moment to mourn, in G. Lewis, S. Gewirtz and J. Clarke (eds) *Rethinking Social Policy*. London: The Open University in association with Sage.

Deacon, A. (1996) Editorial introduction, in F. Field, *Stakeholder Welfare*. London: Institute for Economic Affairs.

Deakin, N. (1987) *The Politics of Welfare*. London: Methuen and Co.

Dean, H. (1989) Disciplinary partitioning and the privatisation of social security, *Critical Social Policy*, 24, 74–82.

Dean, M. (1994) *Critical and Effective Histories: Foucault's Methods and Historical Sociology*. London: Routledge.

Department of Health (1988) *Protecting Children: A Guide for Social Workers Undertaking a Comprehensive Assessment in Cases of Child Protection*. London: HMSO.

Department of Health (1989) *Caring for People: Community Care in the Next Decade and Beyond*. Cm 849. London: HMSO.

Department of Health (1990a) *Community Care in the Next Decade and Beyond*. London: HMSO.

Department of Health (1990b) *The Care Programme Approach for People with a Severe Mental Illness Referred to the Specialist Psychiatric Services*. London: Department of Health.

Department of Health (1991a) *The Patient's Charter*. London: HMSO.

Department of Health (1991b) *Child Abuse. A Study of Inquiry of Reports 1980–1989*. London: HMSO.

Department of Health (1991c) *Assessment Systems and Community Care*. London: HMSO.

Department of Health (1991d) *Care Management and Assessment: Managers' Guide*. London: HMSO.

Department of Health (1991e) *Care Management and Assessment: Practitioners' Guide*. London: HMSO.

Department of Health (1991f) *Working Together under the Children Act 1989: A Guide to Arrangements for Inter-agency Co-operation for the Protection of Children from Abuse*. London: HMSO.

Department of Health (1992) *The Health of the Nation: A Strategy for Health in England*. London: HMSO.

Department of Health (1993) *The Ten Point Plan*. Press release, London.

Department of Health (1994a) *Guidance on the Discharge of Mentally Disordered People and Their Continuing Care in the Community. Health Service Guidelines*. Local Authority Social Services Letter LASSL (94)4. London: Department of Health.

Department of Health (1994b) *Draft Guide to Arrangements for Inter-agency Working for Care and Protection of Severely Mentally Ill People*. London: Department of Health.

Department of Health (1995) *Building Bridges: A Guide to Arrangements for Inter-agency Working for the Care and Protection of Severely Mentally Ill People*. London: The Stationery Office.

Department of Health (1996) *The Spectrum of Care – A Summary of Comprehensive Local Services for People with Mental Health Problems*. HSG (96) 6/LASSL (96) 6. London: The Stationery Office.

Department of Health (1997) *The New NHS: Modern, Dependable*. London: The Stationery Office.

Department of Health (1998a) *Our Healthier Nation: A Contract for Health*. London: The Stationery Office.

Department of Health (1998b) *Modernising Social Services: Promoting Independence, Improving Protection, Raising Standards*. London: The Stationery Office.

Department of Health (1998c) *Modernising Mental Health Services: Safe, Sound and Supportive*. London: Department of Health.

Department of Health (1999a) *Working Together to Safeguard Children – Government Guidance on Inter-agency Co-operation*. London: The Stationery Office.

Department of Health (1999b) *Framework of the Assessment of Children in Need and Their Families (Consultation Draft)*. London: The Stationery Office.

Department of Health (1999c) *Reform of the Mental Health Act 1983: Proposals for Consultation*. London: The Stationery Office.

Department of Health (1999d) *Safer Services: National Confidential Inquiry into Suicide and Homicide by People with Mental Illness*. London: The Stationery Office.

Department of Health (2000) *The NHS Plan: The Government's Response to the Royal Commission on Long Term Care*. London: The Stationery Office.

Department of Health and Home Office (1992a) *Memorandum of Good Practice on Video Recording Interviews with Child Witnesses for Criminal Proceedings*. London: HMSO.

Department of Health and Home Office (1992b) *Review of Health and Social Services for Mentally Disordered Offenders and Others Requiring Similar Services: Final Summary Report*. London: HMSO.

Department of Health and Social Security (1974) *Revised Report of the Working Party on Security in NHS Psychiatric Hospitals*. London: DHSS.

Department of Health and Social Security (1975) *Better Services for the Mentally Ill*. London: HMSO.

Department of Health and Social Security (1976) *Prevention and Health: Everybody's Business*. London: HMSO.

Department of Health and Social Security (1981) *Care in Action: A Handbook of Policies and Priorities for the Health and Social Services*. London: HMSO.

Department of Health and Social Security (1987) *Promoting Better Health: The Government's Programme for Improving Primary Health Care*, Cm 249. London: HMSO.

Department of Health and Social Security (1988) *Working Together: A Guide to Interagency Co-operation for the Protection of Children from Abuse*. London: HMSO.

Department of Social Security (1998) *New Ambitions for Our Country: A New Contract for Welfare*. Green Paper, Cm 3805. London: DSS.

Directors of Social Work in Scotland (1992) *Child Protection Policy, Practice and Procedure*. Edinburgh: HMSO.

Ditchfield, J. (1997) Actuarial prediction and risk assessment, *Prison Service Journal*, 113, 8–13.

Donzelot, J. (1980) *The Policing of Families*. London: Hutchinson.

Douglas, M. (1986) *Risk Acceptability According to the Social Sciences*. London: Routledge and Kegan Paul.

Douglas, M. (1992) *Risk and Blame: Essays in Cultural Theory*. London: Routledge.

Doyal, L. (1993) Human need and the moral right to optimal community care, in J. Bornat, J. Johnson, C. Pereira, D. Pilgrim, F. Williams (eds) *Community Care: A Reader*. Basingstoke: Macmillan Press in association with the Open University.

Doyal, L. and Gough, I. (1991) *A Theory of Human Need*. Basingstoke: Macmillan Press.

Economic and Social Research Council (1993) *Risk and Human Behaviour*. Programme specification. Swindon: ESRC.

Ellis, K. (1993) *Squaring the Circle: User and Carer Participation in Needs Assessment*. York: Joseph Rowntree Foundation.

Ellis, K., Davis, A. and Rummery, K. (1999) Needs assessment, street-level bureaucracy and the new community care, *Social Policy and Administration*, 33(3), 262–80.

Eldridge, J., Kitzinger, J. and Williams, K. (1997) *The Mass Media and Power in Modern Britain*. Oxford: Oxford University Press.

Elliott, L., White, M. and Carvel, J. (2000) Priority no. 1: the NHS (http://www.guardianunlimited.co.uk).

Equinox (2000) The rise and fall of GM. Channel 4, 20 March.

Etzioni, A. (1993) *The Spirit of Community*. New York: Touchstone Books.

Etzioni, A. (1997) *The New Golden Rule*. London: Profile Books.

Exworthy, M. and Powell, M. (2000) Variations on a theme: New Labour, health inequalities and policy failure, in A. Hann (ed.) *Analysing Health Policy*. Aldershot: Ashgate.

Faux, J. (1999) Lost on the third way, *Dissent*, 46(2), 67–76.

Feaviour, P., Peacock, D., Sanderson, H., Bontoff, C. and Wightman, S. (1995) Risk management: score values, *Community Care*, 2–8 November, 28–9.

Fennell, P. (1999) The third way in mental health policy: negative rights, positive rights, and the convention, *Journal of Law and Society*, 26(1), 103–27.

Field, F. (1996) Making welfare work: the underlying principle, in A. Deacon (ed.) *Stakeholder Welfare*. London: IEA Health and Welfare Unit, Choice in Welfare Series, no. 32.

Field, F. (2000) Interview on *World at One*. BBC Radio 4, 27 September.

Finer, Jones C. (1997) The new social policy in Britain, *Social Policy and Administration*, 31(5), 154–70.

Foster, A. (1998) Thinking about risk, in A. Foster and V. Z. Roberts (eds) *Managing Mental Health in the Community: Chaos and Containment*. London: Routledge.

Foster, F. (1995) *Women and the Health Care Industry*. Buckingham: Open University Press.

Foster, P. (1983) *Access to Welfare: An Introduction to Welfare Rationing*. Basingstoke: Macmillan Press.

Foucault, M. (1965) *Madness and Civilization: The History of Insanity in the Age of Reason*. New York: Pantheon.

Foucault, M. (1970) *The Order of Things*. London: Tavistock.

Foucault, M. (1973) *The Birth of the Clinic: An Archaeology of Medical Perception*. London: Tavistock.

Foucault, M. (1977) *Discipline and Punish. The Birth of the Prison*. London: Allen Lane.

Foucault, M. (1978) About the concept of the 'dangerous individual' in 19th century legal psychiatry, *International Journal of Law and Psychiatry*, 1, 1–18.

Foucault, M. (1991) Governmentality, in G. Burchell, C. Gordon and P. Miller (eds) *The Foucault Effect: Studies in Governmentality*. London: Harvester Wheatsheaf.

Freeman, R. (1992) The idea of prevention: a critical review, in S. Scott, G. Williams, S. Platt and H. Thomas (eds) *Private Risks and Public Dangers*. Aldershot: Avebury.

Freudenberg, W. R. (1988) Perceived risk, real risk: social science and the art of probabilistic risk assessment, *Science*, 242 (October), 44–9.

Freudenberg, W. R. (1993) Risk and recreancy: Weber, the division of labour, and the rationality of risk perception, *Social Forces*, 71, 909–32.

Furedi, F. (1997) *Culture of Fear: Risk-taking and the Morality of Low Expectation*. London: Cassell.

Furlong, A. and Cartmel, F. (1997) *Young People and Social Change: Individualization and Risk in Late Modernity*. Buckingham: Open University Press.

Gamble, A. (1988) *The Free Economy and the Strong State*. London and Basingstoke: Macmillan Press.

Giddens, A. (1984) *The Constitution of Society: Outline of the Theory of Structuration*. London and Basingstoke: Macmillan Press.

Giddens, A. (1990) *The Consequences of Modernity*. Cambridge: Polity Press.

Giddens, A. (1991) *Modernity and Self-identity: Self and Society in the Late Modern Age*. Cambridge: Polity Press.

Giddens, A. (1994) Living in a post-traditional society, in U. Beck, A. Giddens and S. Lash (eds) *Reflexive Modernization: Politics, Tradition and Aesthetics in the Modern Social Order*. Cambridge: Polity Press.

Giddens, A. (1998a) Risk society: the context of British politics, in J. Franklin (ed.) *The Politics of Risk Society*. Oxford: Polity Press in association with the Institute for Public Policy Research.

Giddens, A. (1998b) *The Third Way: The Renewal of Social Democracy*. Oxford: Polity Press.

Giddens, A. (1999) *BBC Reith Lectures*. BBC Radio 4.

Giddens, A. (2000) *The Third Way and Its Critics*. Cambridge: Policy Press.

Gladstone, D. (1997) *How to Pay for Health Care: Public and Private Alternatives*. London: IEA Health and Welfare Unit.

Glennerster, H. (1983) *Planning for Priority Groups*. Oxford: Martin Robertson.

Glennerster, H. (1999) A third way? in H. Dean and R. Woods (eds) *Social Policy Review, 11*. Luton: SPA.

Goldsmith, M. (1997) Co-payment: a vehicle for NHS funding enhancement? in D. Gladstone (ed.) *How to Pay for Health Care: Public and Private Alternatives*. London: IEA Health and Welfare Unit.

Gordon, C. (1991) Governmental rationality: an introduction, in G. Burchell, C. Gordon and P. Miller (eds) *The Foucault Effect: Studies in Governmentality*. Hemel Hempstead: Harvester Wheatsheaf.

Gough, I. (1984) *The Political Economy of the Welfare State*. London: Macmillan.

Greco, M. (1993) Psychosomatic subjects and the 'duty to be well': personal agency within medical rationality, *Economy and Society*, 22(3), 357–72.

Green, D. (1985) *Working-class Patients and the Medical Establishment*. Aldershot: Gower/Temple Smith.

Green, D. (1997) From National Health monopoly to National Health guarantee, in D. Gladstone (ed.) *How to Pay for Health Care: Public and Private Alternatives*. London: IEA Health and Welfare Unit.

Green, D. (1998) Mutuality and voluntarism: a 'third way' of welfare reform? in E. Brunsdon, H. Dean and R. Woods (eds) *Social Policy Review 10*. London: SPA.

Green, J. (1995) Accidents and the risk society: some problems with prevention, in R. Bunton, S. Nettleton and R. Burrows (eds) *The Sociology of Health Promotion*. London: Routledge.

Green, J. (1997) *Risk and Misfortune*. London: UCL Press.

Griffiths, Sir G. (1988) *Community Care: Agenda for Action. A Report to the Secretary of State for Social Services*. London: HMSO.

Grounds, A. (1996) *Psychiatry and Public Protection*. Public lecture, annual meeting, Mental Health Commission for Northern Ireland.

Guardian (1999) Hague and Lilley put market in its place, *Guardian*, 21 April, 11.

Guardian (2000a) Doctors snub Blair 'big idea', *Guardian*, 1 June, 1.

Guardian (2000b) Labour stakes credibility on 5 year NHS revolution: reforms at a glance, *Guardian*, 28 July, 1.

Hacking, I. (1987) Was there a probabilistic revolution 1800–1930? in L. Kruger, L. Daston and M. Heidelberger (eds) *The Probabilistic Revolution. Volume 1, Ideas in History*. Cambridge, MA: MIT Press.

Hacking, I. (1990) *The Taming of Chance*. Cambridge: Cambridge University Press.

Hall, S. (1998) The great moving nowhere show, *Marxism Today*, November/December, 9–14.

Hallett, C. and Birchall, E. (1992) *Coordination and Child Protection: A Review of the Literature*. London: HMSO.

Ham, C. (1997) Learning from the tigers: stakeholder health care, in D. Gladstone (ed.) *How to Pay for Health Care: Public and Private Alternatives*. London: IEA Health and Welfare Unit.

Hanily, F. (1999) Policy and legislation in the management of crisis and risk, in T. Ryan (ed.) *Managing Crisis and Risk in Mental Health Nursing*. Cheltenham: Stanley Thornes Publishers.

Hargreaves, I. and Christie, I. (1998) Rethinking retirement, in I. Hargreaves and I. Christie (eds) *Tomorrow's Politics: The Third Way and Beyond*. London: Demos.

Harris, R. (1999) Mental disorder and social order: underlying themes in crime management, in D. Webb and R. Harris (eds) *Mentally Disordered Offenders: Managing People who Nobody Knows*. London: Routledge.

Harris, J. and McDonald, C. (2000) Post-Fordism, the welfare state and the personal social services: a comparison of Australia and Britain, *British Journal of Social Work*, 30, 51–70.

Harris, P. (1999) Public welfare and liberal governance, in A. Petersen, I. Barns, J. Dudley and P. Harris (eds) *Poststructuralism, Citizenship and Social Policy*. London: Routledge.

Harrison, S. and Wood, B. (2000) New Labour's health policy: a 'third way' to organise? in A. Hann (ed.) *Analysing Health Policy*. Aldershot: Ashgate.

Health Committee First Report (1994–5) *Priority Setting in the NHS: Purchasing*. HC 134–1.

Her Majesty's Inspectorate of Probation (1997) Risk management guidance, in Home Office/Association of Chief Officers of Probation, *The Assessment and Management of Risk*. London: Home Office/Association of Chief Officers of Probation, Section 4.

Heron, E. and Dwyer, P. (1999) Doing the right thing: Labour's attempt to forge a new welfare deal between the individual and the state, *Social Policy and Administration*, 33(1), 91–104.

Herring, R. and Thom, B. (1997) The right to take risks: alcohol and older people, *Social Policy and Administration*, 31(3), 233–46.

Heyman, B. (1998) *Risk, Health and Health Care: A Qualitative Approach*. London: Arnold.

Higgs, P. (1998) Risk, governmentality and the reconceptualization of citizenship, in G. Scrambler and P. Higgs (eds) *Modernity, Medicine and Health: Medical Sociology Towards 2000*. London: Routledge.

Hill, M. (1969) The exercise of discretion in the National Assistance Board, *Public Administration*, 47, 75–90.

Hillyard, P. and Watson, S. (1996) Postmodern social policy: a contradiction in terms? *Journal of Social Policy*, 25(3), 321–46.

Home Office (1950) *Children Neglected or Ill-treated in Their Own Homes*. Joint Circular with the Ministry of Education. London: HMSO.

Home Office (1990) *Provision for Mentally Disordered Offenders*. HOC 66/90. London: Home Office.

Home Office (1992) *Directions to the Parole Board under s.32 (6) of the CJA 1991, Annexe A of Circular 85/1992*. London: Home Office.

Home Office (1997) *Sex Offenders Act 1997*. HOC 39/1997. London: Home Office.

Home Office (1998) *The Crime and Disorder Act. Introductory Guide*. London: Home Office.

Home Office and Department of Health and Social Security (1975) *Committee on Mentally Abnormal Offenders (Butler Committee)*. Home Office and Department of Health, Cmnd 6244. London: HMSO.

Home Office and Department of Health (1995) *Mentally Disordered Offenders: Inter-agency Working*. London: Home Office and Department of Health.

Home Office and Department of Health (1999) *Managing Dangerous People with Severe Personality Disorder: Proposals for Policy Development*. London: Home Office and Department of Health.

Home Office, Department of Health, Department of Education and Science and Welsh Office (1991) *Working Together under the Children Act 1989: A Guide to Arrangements for Inter-agency Co-operation for the Protection of Children from Abuse*. London: HMSO.

Hood, C. (1996) Where extremes meet: 'sprat' versus 'shark' in public risk management, in C. Hood and D. K. C. Jones (eds) *Accident and Design: Contemporary Debates in Risk Management*. London: UCL Press.

Hood, C., Jones, D., Pidgeon, N., Turner, B. and Gibson, R. (1992) Risk management, in The Royal Society, *Risk Analysis, Perception and Management*. London: Report of a Royal Society Study Group.

Hood, C. and Jones, D. K. D. (1996) *Accident and Design: Contemporary Debates in Risk Management.* London: UCL Press.

Horizon (2000) Is GM Safe? BBC 2, 9 March.

Horlick-Jones, T. (1996) The problem of blame, in C. Hood and D. K. C. Jones (eds) *Accident and Design: Contemporary Debates in Risk Management.* London: University College London.

Horlick-Jones, T. (1998) Meaning and contextualisation in risk assessment, *Reliability Engineering and System Safety*, 5, 79–89.

Hugman, R. (1994) Social work and case management in the UK: models of professionalism and elderly people, *Ageing and Society*, 14, 237–53.

Hugman, R. (1998) *Social Welfare and Social Value: The Role of the Caring Professions.* Basingstoke: Macmillan.

Hutton, W. (1996) *The State We're In.* London: Vintage.

Isaacs, B. and Evers, H. (1981) *Innovations in the Care of the Elderly.* London: Croom Helm.

Independent on Sunday (2000) Blair: GM may be health risk, *Independent on Sunday*, 27 February, 1.

Jackson, S. (1982) *Childhood and Sexuality.* Oxford: Blackwell Press.

Jackson, S. and Scott, S. (1999) Risk anxiety and the social construction of childhood, in D. Lupton (ed.) *Risk and Sociocultural Theory: New Directions and Perspectives.* Cambridge: Cambridge University Press.

Jasanoff, S. (1993) Bridging the two cultures of risk analysis, *Risk Analysis*, 13(2), 123–9.

Jenkins, S. (1998) It's the doers wot get the blame, *The Sunday Times*, 20 August, Section B, 1.

Jessop, B. (1993) Towards a Schumpeterian welfare state? Preliminary remarks on post-Fordist political economy, *Studies in Political Economy*, 40, 7–39.

Jessop, B. (1994) The transition to a post-Fordist and Schumperterian welfare state, in R. Burrows and B. Loader (eds) *Towards a Post-Fordist Welfare State?* London: Routledge.

Jessop, B. (2000) From the KWNS to the SWPR, in G. Lewis, S. Gerwitz and J. Clarke (eds) *Rethinking Social Policy.* London: Sage and Open University.

Johnson, N. (1999) The personal social services and community care, in M. Powell (ed.) *New Labour, New Welfare? The 'Third Way' in British Social Policy.* Bristol: The Policy Press, University of Bristol.

Johnson, P. (1998a) Historical readings of old age and ageing, in P. Johnson and P. Thane (eds) *Old Age from Antiquity to Post-modernity.* London: Routledge.

Johnson, P. (1998b) Parallel histories of retirement in modern Britain, in P. Johnson and P. Thane (eds) *Old Age from Antiquity to Post-modernity.* London: Routledge.

Jordan, B. (1998) *The New Politics of Welfare.* London: Sage.

Jordan, B. (2000) *Social Work and the Third Way: Tough Love as Social Policy.* London: Sage.

Jowell, R. (1994) *The British Social Attitudes Survey.* 11th report, Dartmouth/SCPR.

Karpf, A. (1988) *Doctoring the Media.* London: Routledge.

Kelly, M. and Charlton, B. (1995) The modern and the post-modern in health promotion, in R. Bunton, S. Nettleton and R. Burrows (eds) *The Sociology of Health Promotion.* London: Routledge.

Kempe, C. H., Silverman, F. N., Steel, B. F., Droegemueller, W. and Silver, H. K. (1962) The battered child syndrome, *Journal of the American Medical Association*, 181, 17–24.

Kemshall, H. (1984) *Defining Clients' Needs in Social Work*. Social Work Monographs. Norwich: University of East Anglia.

Kemshall, H. (1996) *Reviewing Risk: A Review of Research on the Assessment and Management of Risk and Dangerousness: Implications for Policy and Practice in the Probation Service*. London: Home Office.

Kemshall, H. (1998) *Risk in Probation Practice*. Aldershot: Ashgate.

Kemshall, H. (1999) Public perception and the amplification of risk: considerations for the probation service in communicating risk to the public, *VISTA*, 4(3), 185–200.

Kemshall, H. (2000) Transfer of learning: the possibilities and pitfalls of transfer in vocational higher education, in C. Macaulay and V. Cree (eds) *Transfer of Learning: Theory and Practice*. London: Routledge.

Kemshall, H., Parton, N., Walsh, M. and Waterson, J. (1997) Concepts of risk in relation to organisational structure and functioning within the Personal Social Services and Probation, *Social Policy and Administration*, 31(3), 213–32.

Kemshall, H. and Pritchard, J. (eds) (1996) *Good Practice in Risk Assessment and Risk Management, Volume 1*. London: Jessica Kingsley Publishers.

Kemshall, H. and Pritchard, J. (1997) *Good Practice in Risk Assessment and Risk Management, Volume 2: Protection, Rights and Responsibilities*. London: Jessica Kingsley Publishers.

Key, M. (1989) The practice of assessing elders, in O. Stevenson (ed.) *Age and Vulnerability*. London: Edward Arnold.

Kingham, M. (1997) Risk imagery and the AIDS epidemic, in B. Heyman (ed.) *Risk, Health and Health Care: A Qualitative Approach*. London: Arnold.

Kitzinger, J. (1999) Researching risk and the media, *Health Risk and Society*, 1(1), 55–70.

Klein, R. (1989) *The Politics of the National Health Service*, 2nd edn. Harlow: Longman.

Klein, R. (1995) *The New Politics of the National Health Service*. London: Longman.

Klein, R. and Millar, J. (1995) Do-it-yourself social policy, *Social Policy and Administration*, 29, 303–16.

Labour Party (1997) *New Labour because Britain Deserves Better (1997 General Election Manifesto)*. London: Labour Party.

Langan, M. (1990) Community care in the 1990s: the community care White Paper: 'Caring for People', *Critical Social Policy*, 10(2), 58–70.

Langan, M. (1992) Who cares? Women in the mixed economy of welfare, in M. Langan and L. Day (eds) *Women Oppression and Social Work*. London: Routledge.

Langan, M. (1993) New directions in social work, in J. Clarke (ed.) *A Crisis in Care? Challenges to Social Work*. London: Sage in association with Open University Press.

Langan, M. (1998) *Welfare: Needs, Rights and Risks*. London: Open University and Routledge.

Lash, S. (1994) Reflexivity and its doubles: structure, aesthetics, community, in

U. Beck, A. Giddens and S. Lash (eds) *Reflexive Modernization: Politics, Tradition and Aesthetics in the Modern Social Order*. Oxford: Blackwell.

Lavalette, M. and Pratt, A. (eds) (1997) *Social Policy: A Conceptual and Theoretical Introduction*. London: Sage.

Lawrie, C. (1997) Risk: the role and responsibilities of middle managers, in H. Kemshall and J. Pritchard (eds) *Good Practice in Risk Assessment and Risk Management, Volume 1*. London: Jessica Kingsley Publishers.

Lawson, J. (1996) A framework of risk assessment and management for older people, in H. Kemshall and J. Pritchard (eds) *Good Practice in Risk Assessment and Risk Management, Volume 1*. London: Jessica Kingsley Publishers.

Lawson, R. (1993) The new technology of new management in the personal social services, in P. Taylor-Gooby and R. Lawson (eds) *Markets and Managers: New Issues in the Delivery of Welfare*. Buckingham: Open University Press.

Leonard, P. (1997) *Postmodern Welfare*. London: Sage.

Levitt, R. and Wall, A. (1992) *The Reorganised National Health Service*, 4th edn. London: Chapman Hall.

Lewis, J. and Glennerster, H. (1996) *Implementing the New Community Care*. Buckingham: Open University Press.

Littlechild, R. and Blakeney, J. (1996) Risk and older people, in H. Kemshall and J. Pritchard (eds) *Good Practice in Risk Assessment and Risk Management, Volume 1*. London: Jessica Kingsley Publishers.

Littlechild, R. and Glasby, J. (2000) Older people as 'participating patients', in H. Kemshall and R. Littlechild (eds) *User Involvement and Participation in Social Care: Research Informing Practice*. London: Jessica Kingsley Publishers.

Lipsky, M. (1980) *Street-level Bureaucracy*. New York: Russell Sage.

Livesley, B. and Crown, J. (eds) (1992) *Assessing the Needs of Elderly People: Report of a Workshop Held at the Department of Health*. London: Research for Ageing Trust.

London Borough of Brent (1985) *A Child in Trust: The Report of the Panel of Inquiry into the Circumstances Surrounding the Death of Jasmine Beckford*. Presented by members of the Panel of Inquiry, London Borough of Brent.

Lupton, D. (1993) Risk as moral danger: the social and political functions of risk discourse in public health, *International Journal of Health Services*, 23, 425–35.

Lupton, D. (1995) *The Imperative of Health: Public Health and the Regulated Body*. London: Sage.

Lupton, D. (1999) *Risk*. London: Routledge.

McCurry, P. (1999) Decision time on long-term care? *Community Care*, 11–17 March, 8–9.

Macdonald, V. (1996) Focus, *Sunday Telegraph*, 14 April.

MacFarlane, A. (1979) The family, sex and marriage in England 1500–1800, by Laurence Stone, *History and Theory*, 18, 103–26.

Maguire, M., Kemshall, H. and Noaks, L. (2000) *Risk Management of Sexual and Violent Offenders: The Work of Public Protection Panels*. London: Home Office Policing and Reducing Crime Unit.

Manning, N. (2000) Psychiatric diagnosis under conditions of uncertainty: personality disorder, science, and professional legitimacy, *Sociology of Health and Illness*, 22(5), 621–39.

Melling, J. (1999) Accommodating madness: new research in the social history of insanity and institutions, in J. Melling and B. Forsythe (eds) *Insanity, Institutions and Society 1800–1914*. London: Routledge.

Melling, J. and Forsythe, B. (eds) (1999) *Insanity, Institutions and Society 1800–1914*. London: Routledge.

Mental Health Foundation (1994) *Creating Community Care: Report of the Mental Health Foundation Inquiry into Community Care for People with Severe Mental Illness*. London: Mental Health Foundation.

Meredith, B. (1993) *The Community Care Handbook: The New System Explained*. London: Age Concern.

Milburn, A. (2000a) The NHS, cited in P. Barkham, on the Guardian News Unlimited website, 5 May (www.guardianunlimited.co.uk/NHS).

Milburn, A. (2000b) Interview on *Breakfast with Frost*. BBC 1, 4 June.

Miles, A. and Baldwin, T. (2000) Adapt or die, Blair warns NHS. Guardian News Unlimited website (www.guardianunlimited.co.uk/NHS).

Millar, J. and Warman, A. (1996) *Family Obligations in Europe*. London: Family Policy Studies Centre.

Miller, D. and Reilly, J. (1996) Mad cows and Englishmen, *Planet: The Welsh Internationalist*, 117 (June), 118–19.

Miller, P. and Rose, N. (1988) Political rationalities and technologies of government. Paper presented at Colloquium on Language and Politics, University of Helsinki, subsequently published in *Politika*, 1989, in Finnish translation.

Miller, P. and Rose, N. (1990) Governing economic life, *Economy and Society*, 19, 1–13.

MIND (1986) *Finding Our Own Solutions*. London: MIND.

MIND (1999) *Summary of Evidence to House of Commons Home Affairs Committee: Inquiry into the Government's Proposals for Managing Dangerous People with Severe Personality Disorder*. London: MIND.

Mitchell, P. (1997) Rationing debate resurfaces in UK, *Lancet*, 350(9072): 196.

Modern Public Services for Britain (1998) London: Stationery Office, June.

Mooney, G. (1997) Quasi-markets and the mixed economy of welfare, in M. Lavalette and A. Pratt (eds) *Social Policy: A Conceptual and Theoretical Introduction*. London: Sage.

Morgan, C. and Murgatroyd, S. (1994) *Total Quality Management in the Public Sector*. Buckingham: Open University Press.

Moss, P., Dillon, J. and Statham, J. (2000) The 'child in need' and 'the rich child': discourses, constructions of practice, *Critical Social Policy*, 20(2), 233–54.

Muijen, M. (1996) Scare in the community: Britain in moral panic, in T. Heller, J. Reynolds, R. Gomm, R. Mutson and S. Pattison (eds) *Mental Health Matters: A Reader*. London: Macmillan.

Murray, C. (1989) The underclass, *Sunday Times Magazine*, 26 November, 26–45.

Murray, C. (1990) *The Emerging British Underclass*. London: IEA Health and Welfare Unit.

National Association for the Care and Resettlement of Offenders (NACRO) (1998) *Risk and Rights: Mentally Disturbed Offenders and Public Protection*. A report by NACRO's Mental Health Advisory Committee. London: NACRO.

National Audit Office (1994) *Auditing Clinical Care in Scotland*. HC 275. London: National Audit Office.

National Health Service Management Executive (1993) *Risk Management in the Health Service*. London: Department of Health.

National Schizophrenia Fellowship (1989) *Slipping Through the Net*. Kingston-upon-Thames: National Schizophrenia Fellowship.

Neill, J., Sinclair, I., Gorbach, P. and Williams, J. (1988) *A Need for Care? Elderly Applicants for Local Authority Homes*. London: Gower.

Nettleton, S. (1997) Governing the risky self: how to become healthy, wealthy, and wise, in A. Petersen and R. Bunton (eds) *Foucault Health and Medicine*. London: Routledge.

Nettleton, S. and Burrows, R. (1998) Individualisation processes and social policy: insecurity, reflexivity and risk in the restructuring on contemporary British health and housing policies, in J. Carter (ed.) *Postmodernity and the Fragmentation of Welfare*. London: Routledge.

Newman, J. and Clarke, J. (1994) Going about our business? The managerialisation of public services, in J. Clarke, A. Cochrane and E. McLaughlin (eds) *Managing Social Policy*. London: Sage.

Newnes, C. and Holmes, G. (1999) The future of mental health services, in C. Newnes, G. Holmes and C. Dunn (eds) *This is Madness: A Critical Look at Psychiatry and the Future of Mental Health Services*. Ross on Wye: PCCS Books.

NHS Executive (1999) *Effective Care Co-ordination in Mental Health Services: Modernising the Care Programme Approach*. London: NHS Executive and Department of Health.

Norman, A. J. (1980) *Rights and Risks*. London: Centre for Policy on Ageing.

Okell, C. and Butcher, C. H. H. (1969) The battered child syndrome, *Law Society Gazette*, 66(9).

O'Malley, P. (1992) Risk, power and crime prevention, *Economy and Society*, 2(3), 252–75.

O'Malley. P. (1996) Risk and responsibility, in A. Barry, T. Osborne and N. Rose (eds) *Foucault and Political Reason*. London: UCL Press Limited.

Onyett, S. (1992) *Case Management in Mental Health*. London: Chapman Hall.

O'Rourke, M. and Hammond, S. (2000) *Risk Management: Towards Safe, Sound and Supportive Service*. Surrey Hampshire Borders NHS Trust.

Parker, H. (1982) *The Moral Hazard of Social Insurance*. Research Monograph no. 37. London: Institute of Economic Affairs.

Parole Board (1994) *Annual Report*. London: HMSO.

Parsloe, P. (1999) *Risk Assessment in Social Care and Social Work*. London: Jessica Kingsley Publishers.

Parton, N. (1979) The natural history of child abuse: a study in social problem definition, *British Journal of Social Work*, 9, 431–51.

Parton, N. (1991) *Governing the Family: Child Care, Child Protection and the State*. London: Macmillan.

Parton, N. (1994) Problematics of government, (post) modernity and social work, *British Journal of Social Work*, 24(1), 9–32.

Parton, N., Thorpe, D. and Wattam, C. (1997) *Child Protection: Risk and the Moral Order*. Basingstoke: Macmillan Press.

Paton, M. (1999) New Labour's health policy: the new health state, in M. Powell (ed.)

New Labour, New Welfare State? The Third Way in British Social Policy. Bristol: Policy Press, University of Bristol.

Paton, M. (2000) New Labour, new health policy, in A. Hann (ed.) *Analysing Health Policy.* Aldershot: Ashgate.

Percy-Smith, J. (1996) *Needs Assessment in Public Policy.* Buckingham: Open University Press.

Peters, T. J. and Waterman, R. H. (1982) *In Search of Excellence: Lessons from America's Best-run Companies.* London: Harper and Row.

Petersen, A. (1994) Governing images: media constructions of the 'normal', 'healthy' subject, *Media Information Australia*, 72, 32–40.

Petersen, A. (1996) Risk and the regulated self: the discourse of health promotion as politics of uncertainty, *Australian and New Zealand Journal of Sociology*, 32(1), 44–57.

Petersen, A. (1997) Risk, governance and the new public health, in A. Petersen and R. Bunton (eds) *Foucault, Health and Medicine.* London: Routledge.

Petersen, A. (1999) Public health, the new genetics and subjectivity, in A. Petersen, I. Barns, J. Dudley and P. Harris (eds) *Poststructuralism, Citizenship and Social Policy.* London: Routledge.

Petersen, A. and Bunton, R. (eds) (1997) *Foucault Health and Medicine.* London: Routledge.

Petersen, A. and Lupton, D. (1996) *The New Public Health: Health and Self in the Age of Risk.* London: Sage.

Pierson, C. (1994) Continuity and discontinuity in the emergence of the 'post-Fordist' welfare state, in R. Burrows and B. Loader (eds) *Towards a Post-Fordist Welfare State?* London: Routledge.

Pierson, C. (1998) *Beyond the Welfare State*, 2nd edn. Cambridge: Policy Press.

Pilgrim, D. and Johnson, J. (1993) Anthology: policy, in J. Bornat, J. Johnson, C. Pereira, D. Pilgrim and F. Williams (ed.) *Community Care: A Reader.* Basingstoke: Macmillan Press in association with the Open University.

Pilgrim, D. and Rogers, A. (1993) *A Sociology of Mental Health and Madness.* Buckingham: Open University Press.

Pilgrim, D. and Rogers, A. (1999) Mental health policy and the politics of mental health: a three tier analytical framework, *Policy and Politics*, 27(1), 13–24.

Porter, R. (1987) *A Social History of Madness.* London: Weidenfeld and Nicholson.

Powell, M. (ed.) (1999) *New Labour, New Welfare State? The Third Way in British Social Policy.* Bristol: The Policy Press, University of Bristol.

Powell, M. (2000) New labour and the third way in the British welfare state: a new and distinctive approach? *Critical Social Policy*, 20(1), 39–60.

Powell, M. and Hewitt, M. (1998) The end of the welfare state? *Social Policy and Administration*, 32(1), 1–13.

Power, M. (1994) *The Audit Explosion.* London: Demos.

Pratt, A. (1997) Neo-liberalism and social policy, in R. Burrows and B. Loader (eds) *Towards a Post-Fordist Welfare State?* London: Routledge.

Prins, H. (1999) *Will They Do It Again? Risk Assessment and Management in Criminal Justice and Psychiatry.* London: Routledge.

Purdy, M. (1999) The health of which nation? Health, social regulation and the new consensus, in M. Purdy and D. Banks (eds) *Health and Exclusion.* London: Routledge.

Purdy, M. and Banks, D. (1999) Tracing continuity and diversity in health and exclusion, in M. Purdy and D. Banks (eds) *Health and Exclusion*. London: Routledge.

Ramon, S. (ed.) (1991) *Beyond Community Care: Normalisation and Integration Work*. London: Macmillan.

Rayner, S. (1992) Cultural theory and risk analysis, in S. Krimsky and D. Golding (eds) *Social Theories of Risk*. Westport, CT: Praeger.

Reddy, S. (1996) Claims to expert knowledge and the subversion of democracy: the triumph of risk over uncertainty, *Economy and Society*, 25(2), 222–54.

Reder, P., Duncan, S. and Gray, M. (1993) *Beyond Blame: Child Abuse Tragedies Revisited*. London: Routledge.

Ritchie, J., Dick, D. and Lingham, R. (1994) *Report of the Committee of Inquiry into the Care of Christopher Clunis*. London: MIND/COHSE.

Rodger, J. (2000) *From a Welfare State to a Welfare Society: The Changing Context of Social Policy in a Postmodern Era*. Basingstoke and London: Macmillan Press.

Rojek, C., Peacock, G. and Collins, S. (1988) *Social Work and Received Ideas*. London: Routledge.

Rose, N. (1985) *The Psychological Complex: Politics and Society in England 1869–1939*. London: Routledge and Kegan Paul.

Rose, N. (1986a) Psychiatry: the discipline of mental health, in P. Miller and N. Rose (eds) *The Power of Psychiatry*. Cambridge: Polity Press.

Rose, N. (1986b) Law, rights and psychiatry, in P. Miller and N. Rose (eds) *The Power of Psychiatry*. Cambridge: Polity Press.

Rose, N. (1987) Beyond the public/private division: law, power and the family, *Journal of Law and Society*, 14(1), 61–76.

Rose, N. (1990) *Governing the Soul: The Shaping of the Private Self*. London: Routledge.

Rose, N. (1992) Governing the enterprising self, in P. Heelas and M. Morris (eds) *The Values of the Enterprise Culture: The Moral Debate*. London: Unwin Hyman.

Rose, N. (1993) Government, authority and expertise in advanced liberalism, *Economy and Society*, 22(3), 283–98.

Rose, N. (1994) Regulating the social, in M. Valerde (ed.) *Radically Re-thinking Regulation*. Workshop report. Toronto: Centre of Criminology, University of Toronto.

Rose, N. (1996) Governing 'advanced' liberal democracies, in A. Barry, T. Osborne and N. Rose (eds) *Foucault and Political Reason: Liberalism, Neo-liberalism and Rationalities of Government*. London: UCL Press.

Rose, N. (2000) Government and control, *British Journal of Criminology*, 40, 321–39.

Rose, N. and Miller, P. (1992) Political power beyond the state: problematics of government, *British Journal of Sociology*, 43(24), 173–205.

Rowe, M. D. (1977) *An Anatomy of Risk*. Chichester: John Wiley and Sons.

Rowntree, B. S. (1947) *Old People: Report of a Survey Committee on the Problems of Ageing and Care of Old People*. London: Nuffield Foundation.

Royal College of Psychiatrists (1993) Press release. London.

Royal College of Psychiatrists' Working Group on the Definition and Treatment of Severe Personality Disorder (1999) *Offenders with Severe Personality Disorder*. Council Report CR 71. London: Gaskell.

Royal Commission on the National Health Service (1979) *The Merrison Report.* Cmnd 7615. London: HMSO.

Royal Commission on Long-term Care for the Elderly (1999) *With Respect to Old Age.* London: The Stationery Office.

Royal Society Study Group (1983) *Royal Society.* London: Royal Society.

Royal Society Study Group (1992) *Risk: Analysis, Perception and Management. Report of a Royal Society Study Group.* London: Royal Society.

Ryan, A. (1999) Britain: re-cycling the third way, *Dissent,* 46(2), 77–80.

Ryan, P. (1999) *Assertive Outreach in Mental Health.* Nursing Times Clinical Monographs 35. London: Nursing Times Monographs.

Ryan, P., Ford, R., Beadsmore, A. and Muijen, M. (1999) The enduring relevance of case management, *British Journal of Social Work,* 29, 97–125.

Ryan, T. (1996) Risk management and people with mental health problems, in H. Kemshall and J. Pritchard (eds) *Good Practice in Risk Assessment and Risk Management, Volume 1.* London: Jessica Kingsley Publishers.

Ryan, T. (2000) Exploring the risk management strategies of mental health service users, *Health, Risk and Society,* 2(3), 267–82.

Saraga, E. (1993) Child abuse, in R. Dallos and E. McLaughlin (eds) *Social Problems and the Family.* London: Sage.

Saunders, P. (1993) Citizenship in a liberal society, in B. Turner (ed.) *Citizenship and Social Theory.* London: Sage.

Scrambler, G. and Higgs, P. (eds) (1998) *Modernity, Medicine and Health: Medical Sociology towards 2000.* London: Routledge.

Scott, S. and Williams, G. (1991) Introduction, in S. Scott, G. Williams, S. Platt and H. Thomas (eds) *Private Risks and Public Dangers.* Aldershot: Avebury.

Scull, A. (1979) *Museums of Madness.* London: Allen Lane.

Scull, A. (1993) Museums of madness revisited, *Social History of Madness,* 6(2), 3–23.

Seebohm, F. (1968) *Report of the Committee on Local Authority and Allied Personal Social Services.* Cmnd 3703. London: HMSO.

Sheppard, D. (1995) *Learning the Lessons: Mental Health Inquiry Reports Published in England and Wales between 1969 and 1994 and Their Recommendations for Improving Practice.* London: Zito Trust.

Sheppard, D. (1996) *Learning the Lessons: Mental Health Inquiry Reports Published in England and Wales between 1969 and 1994 and Their Recommendations for Improving Practice,* 2nd edn. London: Zito Trust.

Sheppard, D. (1997) *Mental Health Inquiries Published During 1997.* Institute of Mental Health Law, Internet publication.

Sheppard, D. (1998) *Mental Health Inquiries Published During 1998.* Institute of Mental Health Law, Internet publication.

Shorter, E. (1997) *A History of Psychiatry: From the Era of the Asylum to the Age of Prozac.* Chichester: John Wiley and Sons.

Simon, J. (1987) The emergence of a risk society: Insurance, law, and the state, *Socialist Review,* 95, 61–89.

Skolbekken, J. (1995) The risk epidemic in medical journals, *Social Science and Medicine,* 40(3), 291–305.

Slovic, P. (1992) Perception of risks: reflections on the psychometric paradigm, in S. Krimsky and D. Golding (eds) *Social Theories of Risk.* Westport, CT: Praeger.

Smart, B. (1993) *Postmodernity*. London: Routledge.

Smith, G. (1980) *Social Need: Policy, Practice and Research*. London: Routledge and Kegan Paul.

Social Services Inspectorate (1991) *Inspection of Child Protection Cases in Rochdale*. Manchester: Department of Health.

Social Services Inspectorate (1993) *Developing Quality Standards for Home Support (A Handbook for Social Services Managers, Inspectors and Users of Services and Their Relatives and Friends)*. London: Social Services Inspectorate, Department of Health.

Social Services Inspectorate (1995) *Partners in Caring. The Fifth Annual Report of the Chief Inspector Social Services Inspectorate 1994/5*. London: HMSO.

Spokes, J., Pare, M. and Royle, G. (1988) *Report of the Committee of Inquiry into the Care and After-care of Miss Sharon Campbell*. London: HMSO.

Steele, L. (1999) Family fortunes, *Community Care*, 4–10 March, 18–19.

Steuer, M. (1998) A little too risky, *London School of Economics Magazine*, 10, 15–16.

Stone, L. (1977) *The Family, Sex and Marriage in England 1500–1800*. London: Weidenfeld and Nicholson.

Strong, P. (1990) Epidemic psychology: a model, *Sociology of Health and Illness*, 12, 249–59.

Tait, E. J. and Levidow, L. (1992) Proactive and reactive approaches to risk regulation: the case of biotechnology, *Futures*, 24 April, 219–31.

Taylor, R. (2000) Blair warns NHS workers to be braced for change (www.guardianunlimited.co.uk/NHS).

Taylor-Gooby, P. (2000a) The future of social policy, in J. Baldock, N. Manning, S. Miller and S. Vickerstaff (eds) *Social Policy*. Oxford: Oxford University Press.

Taylor-Gooby, P. (2000b) *Risk, Trust and Welfare*. Basingstoke and London: Macmillan Press.

Taylor-Gooby, P., Dean, H., Munro, M. and Parker, G. (1999) Risk and the welfare state, *British Journal of Sociology*, 50(2), 177–95.

Thompson, S. and Hoggett, P. (1996) Universalism, selectivism and particularism, *Critical Social Policy*, 16, 21–43.

Thompson, M. and Wildavsky, A. (1982) A proposal to create a cultural theory of risk, in H. C. Kunreuther and E. V. Ley (eds) *The Risk Analysis Controversy: An Institutional Perspective*. New York: Springer-Verlag.

Titmuss, R. (1963) *Essays on the Welfare State*, 2nd edn. London: Allen and Unwin.

Titmuss, R. (1968) *A Commitment to Welfare*. London: Allen and Unwin.

Titmuss, R. (1974) *Social Policy: An Introduction*. London: Allen and Unwin.

Tomlinson, D. (1991) *Utopia, Community Care and the Retreat from the Asylums*. Buckingham: Open University Press.

Townsend, P. (1993) The structured dependency of the elderly, in J. Bornat, J. Johnson, C. Pereira, D. Pilgrim and F. Williams (eds) *Community Care: A Reader*. Basingstoke: Macmillan Press in association with the Open University.

Toynbee, P. (2000) An end to waiting – that's a promise to the health service, *Guardian*, 31 May, 22.

Turner, B. (1997) Foreword: from governmentality to risk, some reflections on Foucault's contribution to medical sociology, in A. Petersen and R. Bunton (eds) *Foucault Health and Medicine*. London: Routledge.

Waldby, C. (1996) *AIDS and the Body Politic*. London: Routledge.

Walby, S. and Greenwell, J. (1994) Managing the National Health Service, in J. Clarke, A. Cochrane and E. McLaughlin (eds) *Managing Social Policy*. London: Sage.

Walker, A. (1993) Community care policy: from consensus to conflict, in J. Bornat, J. Johnson, C. Pereira, D. Pilgrim and F. Williams (eds) *Community Care: A Reader*. Basingstoke: Macmillan Press in association with the Open University.

Wall, A. and Owen, B. (1999) *Health Policy: Health Care and the NHS*. Gildredge Social Policy Series. East Sussex: Gildredge Press Ltd.

Wapshott, N. and Brock, G. (1983) *Thatcher*. London: Futura.

Wildavsky, A. (1988) *Searching for Safety*. New Brunswick, NJ: Transaction Books.

Wilkinson, A. (1997) Improving risk based communications and decision making, *Journal of Petroleum Engineers*, 949, 936–43.

Wistow, G., Knapp, M., Hard, B. and Allen, C. (1994) *Social Care in a Mixed Economy*. Buckingham: Open University.

Wright Mills, C. (1970) *The Sociological Imagination*. Harmondsworth: Pelican Books.

Wynne, B. (1982) *Rationality and Ritual: The Windscale Inquiry and Nuclear Decisions in Britain*. London: British Society for the History of Science.

Wynne, B. (1992) Risk and social learning: reification to learning, in S. Krimsky and D. Golding (eds) *Social Theories of Risk*. Westport, CT: Praeger.

Wynne, B. (1996) May the sheep safely graze? A reflexive view of the expert–lay knowledge divide, in S. Lash, B. Szerszinski and B. Wynne (eds) *Risk, Environment and Modernity: Towards a New Ecology*. London: Sage.

Wyre, R. (1997) Marked for life, *Community Care*, 20–26 February, 26–7.

Index

COMPARATIVE SOCIAL POLICY
THEORY AND RESEARCH

Patricia Kennett

- What are the social policy processes and outcomes across different societies?
- How are these shaped by social and economic conditions?
- What are the limitations and potential of cross-national research?

Comparative Social Policy explores the new context of social policy and considers how cross-national theory and research can respond to the challenges facing welfare. These challenges include changing demographic trends and economic conditions which have been accompanied by the emergence of new needs and risks within and across societies. This book extends and deepens cross-national research by exploring the theoretical and conceptual frameworks through which social policy and welfare systems have been understood. It critically examines different policy processes and welfare outcomes, as well as the ethnocentricism and cultural imperialism which has permeated cross-national epistemology and methodology. The author concludes by reflecting on how cross-national research can illuminate the complex and diverse processes leading to discrimination and inequality across borders. This leads to consideration of how it can contribute to the implementation of welfare provision appropriate to the social and economic conditions of contemporary societies. *Comparative Social Policy* is an essential text for undergraduate and masters level students of social policy, and an invaluable reference for researchers embarking on cross-national social research.

Contents
Introduction – Globalization, supranationalism and social policy – Defining and constructing the research process – Theory and analysis in cross-national social policy research – Development, social welfare and cross-national analysis – Ethnicity, gender and the boundaries of citizenship – Australia, Britain and Japan – The future of comparative social policy research – Notes – Glossary – Bibliography.

192pp   0 335 20123 7 (Paperback)   0 335 20124 5 (Hardback)

EDUCATION IN A POST-WELFARE SOCIETY

Sally Tomlinson

'This book provides a context for understanding educational policies which is currently missing from education and social policy courses. It should be compulsory reading,'

Len Barton, University of Sheffield

- What have been the positive and negative effects of education reforms in recent years?
- Why are the moderate successes of state education unrecognized and education portrayed as 'failing' or in crisis?
- How has the reproduction of privilege by education persisted despite a rhetoric of equality and inclusion?

Education in a Post-welfare Society provides a concise and critical overview of education policy, as government in Britain has moved from creating a welfare state to promoting a post-welfare society dominated by private enterprise and competitive markets. Concentrating particularly on the past twenty years, Sally Tomlinson places in context the avalanche of legislation and documentation that has re-formed education into a competitive enterprise in which young people 'learn to compete'. She also demonstrates how a relatively decentralized education system became a system in which funding, teaching and curriculum were centrally controlled, and education narrowed to an economic function. Chronologies of education acts, reports and initiatives are provided at the beginning of the first six chapters. Major legislation is summarized, and an extensive bibliography and annotated suggestions for further reading provide additional guidance. The result is an invaluable resource for students of social policy and education; as well as educational researchers and professionals.

Contents
Introduction – Social democratic consensus? Education 1945–79 – Market forces gather: education 1980–7 – Creating competition: education 1988–94 – The consequences of competition: education 1994–7 – New Labour and education: 1997–2000 – Centralizing lifelong learning – Education and the middle classes – Equity issues: race and gender – Education and the economy – Conclusion: Education in a post-welfare society – References – Index.

224pp   0 335 20288 8 (Paperback)   0 335 20289 6 (Hardback)

openup

ideas and understanding
in social science

www.**openup**.co.uk

**Browse, search and
order online**

**Download detailed
title information and
sample chapters***

*for selected titles

www.**openup**.co.uk